INDIA UNDER DALHOUSIE AND CANNING

INDIA UNDER DALHOUSIE AND CANNING

DUKE OF ARG GEORGE DOUGLAS CAMPBELL

GYAN

Published by

GYAN

Gyan Publishing House
5, Ansari Road
Daryaganj, New Delhi-110002
Phone: 011-47034999, 9811692060
E-mail: books@gyanbooks.com

Distribution Network
gyanbooks.com
India, USA, Canada, UK, Australia

ISBN: 978-93-7097-292-6 (PB)

First Published, 1865

2nd Impression 2025

Printed at: Gyan Press, Delhi.

INDIA UNDER DALHOUSIE AND CANNING
Author: DUKE OF ARG GEORGE DOUGLAS CAMPBELL

DALHOUSIE AND CANNING.

INDIA

UNDER

DALHOUSIE AND CANNING.

BY

THE DUKE OF ARGYLL.

FROM THE EDINBURGH REVIEW OF JANUARY AND APRIL 1863.

LONDON:
LONGMAN, GREEN, LONGMAN, ROBERTS, & GREEN.
1865.

PREFACE.

THE VIOLENT REACTIONS of feeling and opinion which arose out of the Great Indian Mutiny are now beginning to subside. Time and reflection are sifting the conclusions which were drawn from that event in moments of agony and anger and alarm. Some rash inferences have already almost faded from the public mind; and there are others still popular which are destined not less certainly to disappear. It is the duty of those who have had any special opportunities of observation, either as regards the course of events or as regards the action of the Government, to contribute what they can to the full discussion of the subject. Having been a member of the Cabinet which decided on the Annexation of Oude, and decided, too, not only on the doing of it but substantially on the manner in which it should be done, I have often been astonished by the ignorant injustice with which, on account of this transaction, the memory of Lord Dalhousie has been assailed. It is only very lately that this injustice has come to be acknowledged or understood: yet all the facts have been accessible to the public for many years. "Blue Books" may not be light reading; but those, at least, who undertake to pass judgment on the conduct of public men are bound to know something of the authentic documents in which that conduct, with the reasons which determined it, are recorded. In the case of the Indian Government this duty is the more easy, and the neglect of it is the less excusable, since it is the custom of that Government to record its decisions, with the dissents of every individual member, in elaborate Minutes, often very able, and always exhausting every fact and every argument on either side. The following pages have been written, so far as regards the narrative of political transactions, mainly from those materials. In almost every case in which I have had occasion to consult them, I have found how unsafe it would have been to trust to any less authentic sources of information.

The misconceptions which prevailed till lately in the case of Oude are not broader than the misconceptions which still prevail in respect to several other acts of Lord Dalhousie's Administration. The truth is that such errors are very apt to establish on their own behalf a sort of Reign of Terror. Writers who know, or who ought to know the facts, are deterred from stating them, by the fear of being suspected of heresy on some established dogma of the popular creed. I had hoped better things of Mr. Arnold's work on "Dalhousie's Administration of British India." If Historians of any class are specially bound to an impartial treatment of their subject, it is that class whose works partake largely of the character of Biography. At least, it may be expected of them that they will state the facts in the light in which they were seen by those whose conduct they have undertaken to record, and whose memory is for a time in their keeping. How far Mr. Arnold has performed this duty for Lord Dalhousie—in the cases, for example, of the Annexations of Sattara, of Jhansi, and of Nagpore —I leave to the judgment of those who choose to compare his narrative (if such it can be called) with the account they will find in the Parliamentary Papers. The total omission of many of the most important facts, and the omission, not less unjust, of any adequate attempt even to set forth Lord Dalhousie's reasoning, is a conspicuous failure in historical truth and in biographical fidelity. Nor is this fault atoned for by the allegiance which Mr. Arnold so anxiously professes to some great principle of morality which was not evident to a Statesman of as high honour as ever ruled in India, to the great majority of his Council, to the Court of Directors, or to the members of the Queen's Government at Home.

Mr. Kaye is a writer of much ability, and possessing large knowledge of his subject. But he has some preconceived theories to maintain, and of these he never loses sight. His narratives are always woven so as to bring out a certain pattern; and threads of a colour which do not suit that pattern have not much chance of being taken up. It is because I have been led to form different conclusions from those which have prevailed of late on some important questions connected with the recent History of India, that I now republish these Essays in a separate form. I have the satisfaction of knowing that most of the views here taken had the approval of the late Sir George C. Lewis, whose knowledge on this as well as on so many other subjects was as large and accurate as his judgment was always thoroughly free from prejudice.

ARGYLL.

INDIA UNDER LORD DALHOUSIE.

THE DEATH, in rapid succession, of the last Governor-General and of the first Viceroy of India closes, with sad completeness, the series of great events and great changes which must always be inseparably connected with the names of Dalhousie and of Canning. The period of their Government constitutes an epoch by itself. Our Indian Empire has indeed been, from the first, a very rapid growth: but these two Administrations have seen a double portion of every difficulty, of every danger, and of every triumph which, during the previous century, had tried and confirmed our rule. We propose to review the course of those fourteen memorable years, and to estimate the results which they have bequeathed to us and to future times. It ought now to be possible to do this with a near approach to truth. A whole age seems already to have passed since the Sutlej was the boundary of British India, since the Sepoy was its main defence, and since its Government was still "The Company." And then—one great source of error exists no longer. The personal antagonism which never fails to affect, more or less, the judgment of contemporaries on the conduct of living statesmen, is not generally an antagonism which survives the grave; and as regards these two men—so different, yet both so remarkable—who, during that time, represented the name and fame of England in the East, we can measure very fairly, if we choose to do so, the various merits of their policy, and the different directions of their success.

Lord Dalhousie landed in India early in January 1848. He was a Civilian, with no other official experience than such as had been acquired at the Board of Trade. He came to take the command of a great military Empire out of the hands of a Soldier, who was the comrade and the friend of Wellington, and who, in the tremendous battles of the Sutlej, had found enough to task to the utmost even his knowledge and resource in war. But the universal expectation then was that Lord Dalhousie's reign would be a reign of peace. Strange as this expectation must appear to us, who know what followed, it was, perhaps, not unnatural at the time. At Ferozeshah the fate of India had trembled in the balance; and even now it is hardly possible to read, without holding our breath, the account of those hours of night, when, after a bloody and doubtful contest, Hardinge and Gough went round their decimated battalions telling them that at break of day the bayonet must decide their fate. But that morning charge had been so well delivered, followed by the victory of Aliwal, and the "crowning mercy" of Sobraon, that England believed the Khalsa Army to be broken and destroyed, and the Empire of Runjeet Singh to have passed conclusively into the number of dependent States. Yet barely three months had passed from Lord Dalhousie's landing in the Hooghly, when the murder of Anderson and Agnew, at Mooltan, gave token of all that commonly follows such symptoms in the East. Then came a long series of those deeds of which the history of British India is so full, and of which no other history can produce the like. Single officers—at distant stations, alone, unsupported, in the midst of waverers and fanatics and traitors—by courage, and command, and indomitable determination, as well as by infinite address, kept at bay for many months, with mere handfuls of men, all the various armies of Singhs and Sirdars, and Ameers and Khans. But in spite of Edwardes and Cortlandt, and Abbott and Nicholson, and Lake and Herbert and Lawrence, the tide of rebellion swelled, till, at Chillianwalla, it broke with a vengeance on the Army of Lord Gough.

Such was the greeting which awaited the new Governor-General when, on the first anniversary after his arrival in India, he reached the scene of action on the frontier. After a bloody action, characterised by circumstances of extreme danger, and of some discredit, the British army had enough to do to maintain itself on the field of battle. Salvos from the enemy's artillery gave vent to an exultation which was justified by the capture of four English standards and two English guns. Who does not remember how that salute sounded in our ears at home; and how the Government and people, with one voice, called for the man to whose genius they already owed their latest conquest in the East? Long before Sir Charles Napier, however, had reached the Punjaub, Lord Gough had retrieved his credit as a general: and that onward march, which has known so few halts, had carried the British Forces in triumph beyond Lahore. At Goojerat the Sikh Army was finally routed; and the rapid pursuit by General Gilbert was rewarded, at Rawul Pindee, on the 12th of March 1848, by the surrender of the only Body which remained unbroken. Thirty-five great Feudatories of the Punjaub, and 15,000 men, laid down their arms. Finally, the Affghans, who had been called into alliance by the Sikhs, were "chased with ignominy" beyond Peshawur. The war was ended. On the 28th of March, the young Maharajah was called to resign a sceptre which only one hand in India had now the right or the power to wield. A Proclamation, issued on the following day by Lord Dalhousie, announced that the great Country of the Five Rivers was now an English Province, and that the frontiers of British India extended beyond the Indus to the foot of the mountains of Affghanistan.

The Punjaub is not the last, but it is the most important acquisition which our Indian Empire has received since the days of Wellesley. There is no need to defend that acquisition in point of right, and as little need now to support it in respect to policy. The right never has admitted, and never could admit, of rational doubt. The policy has received from late events a memorable vindication. But as this first great act of Lord Dalhousie's Administration brings before us at the very outset of his career that which has been called his "Policy of Annexation," we shall at once pursue this subject to the close of his rule in India. It is of paramount importance, with reference both to the history of those years, and to the history of the years which followed.

It is indeed true that the annexation of the Punjaub proved to be the first of a series of annexations. Beyond all doubt, one of the most prominent features of the period which we are now reviewing is the great enlargement of our direct dominion which was effected in it. "During the eight years over which we now look back," said Lord Dalhousie, on leaving India, "the British territories in the East have been largely increased. Within that time, four Kingdoms have passed under the sceptre of the Queen of England; and various Chieftainships and separate tracts have been brought under her sway." What is not true is precisely that which is most commonly believed, viz. that this was the result of a policy preconceived and deliberately pursued. No policy was, or could be formed, applicable to the very different circumstances which, in these various cases, terminated in a like result. It has been the same always. A few Forts and Factories, at distant points of the Indian coast, have, within the span almost of a single human life, gathered around them, as round the germs of an organic growth, all the Provinces of Akbar and Aurungzebe. Yet neither Clive nor Warren Hastings, nor Lord Cornwallis nor Lord Wellesley, nor Lord Hastings nor Lord William

Bentinck, nor Lord Ellenborough nor Lord Dalhousie, ever acted on a "Policy of Annexation." But they all annexed. The constancy of the result does, indeed, indicate a cause as constant to explain it. But that cause lies deeper than the policy of statesmen. The truth is that their will has been generally overruled, and compelled to take a new direction. The annexation of the Punjaub is a signal instance. It was the abandonment—the forced abandonment—of a settled plan, approved by Lord Dalhousie, and which he came to India fully determined to maintain. What that plan was, how it came to be proposed, and why it was abandoned, are questions which well illustrate both the features which have been constant and the features which have greatly varied, in our final dealings with the Native Monarchies of India.

It may be justly said of the Kingdom of the Punjaub, that it was quite as deserving our respect as any State with which we had come in contact in the East. It was not ancient; on the contrary, it was younger than our own dominion in Bengal. It was the creation of the last forty years, and the work of a single man. But it had been founded by courage and ability, and it was ruled with prudence and success. Accordingly, the relations which Runjeet Singh cultivated with us, and the relations which we cultivated with Runjeet Singh, were those of mutual friendship and respect. Whilst yet a young man, and when his dominion was as yet incomplete, he had seen the Army of Lord Lake sweep across his country, in pursuit of Holkar. He had seen, too, his own sturdy soldiers give way before the disciplined resolution of Metcalfe's small escort; and with keen and just perception he had formed his estimate of our character and of our power. Nor was our policy towards the Ruler of the Sikhs less firmly based on the doctrine then held as to our own interest. Traditions of the Dooranee Empire, actual experience in the earlier days of "The Company," and the well-known military habits of the races of Northern India, had all contributed to impress the notion upon Indian statesmen that the most formidable danger we had to fear was from the Mohammedan races beyond the Indus. The nucleus of the Sikh people was Hindoo, and the Sikh Kingdom represented the fanaticism of a Hindoo sect. It formed, therefore, precisely such a barrier as India was supposed to want. So entirely was the Punjaub thought to lie beyond the horizon of our possible acquisitions—so little jealous were we of its increasing power—that we seem to have forgotten, in favour of the "Lion of Lahore," one cardinal principle of our policy with all native States. The employment of European officers, not being subjects of the British Crown, by native Princes, was a thing which, above all others, the Government at Calcutta would never tolerate. A well-founded dread of the consequences of such alliance between native courage and the discipline of Europe had been born and bred in every servant of the Company, since the days of Clive and of Dupleix. Yet this was allowed to Runjeet, apparently without remonstrance or alarm. These were all special circumstances in our relations with the Punjaub. But then came a change, bringing to the surface those deeper tendencies which had been for a time concealed, and which soon compelled us to deal with the Successors of Runjeet as we had long before dealt with the Lieutenants of the Mogul. The Government of Runjeet, like so many other Governments in the East, was the government of one man. When he died it fell to pieces. Nothing remained but a powerful Army, without a head to lead or a hand to control it.

From that moment our relations with the Sikhs were complicated with all the difficulties from which there never has been any escape—but one. Yet the Indian Government tried anxiously to find another. The well-known intermediate step was taken, with a desire, more than usually sincere, that it might be final. When, after the first attack of the Khalsa troops, victory had placed the Punjaub at the feet of Lord Hardinge, he deliberately determined to maintain its native Crown and Government. Then came another stage in the invariable process. Without our help the Government could not be maintained at all. The Crown of Runjeet had descended to a child, and the Regency knew that they could not control the Sikhs. They implored the Governor-General not to withdraw his Army from Lahore. Lord Hardinge knew only too well what would be the result of compliance with this request. He had lately come from Oude, where a native Government, rotten to the core, had long been supported by our arms; and he had seen, with indignation and remorse, the terrible effects upon the people of this alliance between British strength and native corruption. Already, during the few months he had been at Lahore, our officers had been the witnesses of gross acts of corruption and injustice. "Considerations of humanity," said Lord Hardinge, "to individuals would be no plea for employing British bayonets in perpetuating the rule of a native State, and enabling such a Government to oppress the people." The Governor-General was determined, therefore, that if our support were indispensably required, it should be given only on one condition, and that was, that the government of the Province should be delivered altogether into the hands of the British Authorities. To these terms the Durbar assented; and it was agreed that, during the minority of the Maharajah, the government should be administered, in his name, by the Resident, with unlimited authority in all matters of administration.

This was the experiment which, though conducted with all the wisdom and faithfulness of Henry Lawrence, ended in what was called the rebellion of the Sikhs, and the second Sikh war. The causes of the failure are evident enough. Apart from the special dangers, in this case, from the warlike character of the Sikhs, and from the facility with which the elements of a formidable Army could be collected from the disbanded Khalsa, there were other causes which belonged to the position we had thus been contented to assume. We were governing the country only too well for the interests of rival factions; but we were governing it, not in our own name, but in the name of the Maharajah. The Sirdars of the Punjaub were not likely to believe that a course so familiar to themselves was determined by motives and intentions so different from their own. It was the usual course taken by Usurpers in the East. Nowhere does the authority of great names last longer—nowhere have the puppets who inherit them been more extensively employed. To take possession of the person of the reigning Sovereign, and plunder in his name—this had long been the goal of successful violence at Delhi and Lucknow, and it promised to be almost as fruitful at Lahore. In this game—as it must have appeared to the Sikh Chiefs—the "Feringhees" had played successfully; but there was no possible reason why those who had been beaten should not try their luck again. We did not pretend to any authority of our own; and the measure of our self-assertion was, to them, the measure of our right. In the vigorous paper in which Lord Dalhousie announced his determination to the Directors, he remarks and dwells upon the fact, that the rebellion was not a rebellion against the young Maharajah, but against the "Feringhees" who sheltered their usurpation under his authority and name. He declares that he had hitherto approved the policy of Lord Hardinge, and had come to India impressed with the inexpediency of extending territory. But every hope under which he had refrained from exercising the full rights of conquest had broken down. If the Sikh Kingdom could be reconstituted as a strong Government, it was now clear that it would be more dangerous than the Affghans, against whom it had been cherished as a bulwark. The attempt to rule it ourselves, under the nominal authority of its native Sovereign, had resulted in another dangerous and bloody war. Nothing remained but that complete incorporation with the rest of our dominions, which could alone make our power effectual, by rendering our authority complete.

We pass from this case of annexation with only one remark. The history of the world presents no more splendid example of deserved success than the administration of the Punjaub under Lord Dalhousie. It displayed the highest virtues of a conquering and ruling race. Beyond all doubt, the success of that Government was largely due to the personal character of those by whom it was conducted; and especially to the character of that remarkable man who, as Chief Commissioner of the Punjaub, has won for himself an immortal name. It is only just to Lord Hardinge to record that the first selection of John Lawrence from a subordinate position was a selection made by his sagacity. He appointed Lawrence to the charge of the Trans-Sutlej Territory—a portion of the Sikh territory which Lord Hardinge annexed at the close of the first Sikh campaign. But the promotion of Lawrence to the Punjaub was the work of Lord Dalhousie; and during the whole period of his Government the Governor-General extended to the Chief Commissioner and his colleagues an active and cordial support. No larger confidence was ever given, as none was ever more deserved; and the seal was set to its reward, when, a few years later, the men who had confronted our power, on almost equal terms, at Ferozeshah and Chillianwalla, were found yoked to our service, with incomparable fidelity, in the attack on Delhi and in the defence of the Alumbagh.

The first great act of Lord Dalhousie's Administration stands in such close connection with his last, that we pass at once to the annexation of Oude. The Indian Government had long occupied precisely that relation to the Ruler and people of Oude which we have seen Lord Hardinge so determined to repudiate in respect to the people and Government of the Punjaub. For more than eighty years the Company and its officers had maintained the policy of non-annexation with perseverance, but with increasing hesitation and remorse. They had yoked their strength to the service of a Native Government, whose ineradicable vices had, from the first moments of its existence, been conspicuous even among the vicious Governments of the East. Those vices had not arisen from our interference; they were of genuine native growth; but they had secured under our protection an impunity which they could never have otherwise enjoyed. It is now very nearly a hundred years since the forces of Shujah-ood-Dowlah were scattered on the field of Buxar, and since the army of Carnac took possession of Lucknow. Oude then belonged by right of conquest to the Anglo-Indian Government; but the policy of the Company was at that time adverse to the assumption of any avowed Sovereignty, even in the Provinces which they had made their own. That policy was founded on motives which are almost forgotten now. They dreaded the rivalry of other European Powers; they dreaded especially the interference of Parliament and the Crown; and they had a just presentiment that the possession of territorial revenues would ultimately interfere with that monopoly in trade to which they trusted as their great source of wealth. When Clive, on his return to India in 1765, found it essential to assume on behalf of the Company that avowed right of collection and administration without which there could be no check on a system of universal plunder, his decision soon elicited from the Directors the unavailing but sagacious reflection, "Should there be occasion for any military operations, it will be found we have not altered our situation for the better, but have only exchanged a certain profit in commerce for a precarious one in revenue."

But there was no escape from that Imperial position which was being forced upon the Company faster than they were willing or able to accept it. All that could be done was to maintain the Princes whom their officers had been compelled to conquer; but to maintain them on conditions which should make them dependent, and, if possible, should make them profitable. Hence the whole system of Provinces subdued but not appropriated,—of Princes who were treated as subjects yet addressed as Sovereigns, and of "Treaties" which expressed nothing but the will of a Superior imposing on his Vassal so much as for the time it was thought expedient to require. And so Clive, in refusing to keep possession of Oude in 1765, took care to provide for the new relations which it was essential to establish by a "treaty" which left it virtually dependent. The victory of Buxar, and this first "treaty" by which it was followed, are the foundations of all our subsequent dealings with Oude. From that day till its final annexation, its native Rulers existed not only upon our sufferance but by our protection. The intermediate steps were slow, but regular, and not to be avoided. A British Resident was established at Lucknow. He authoritatively decided between rival claimants to the Musnud. One was pulled down, and another was set up. Mutinies in the Army were suppressed by the Company's battalions. Then came the usual history of a Government at once powerless and hopelessly corrupt,—the revenues dissipated; the subsidies in arrear; debt, and the increasing dependence which belongs to the position of a debtor. Meanwhile came that great change which arose when the English Parliament awoke to the fact, that the "Company of Merchants trading to the East Indies" were becoming territorial Sovereigns, and were setting their feet on the necks of Kings. From that day statesmen trained in the public life of England, and virtually selected by the Crown, have been responsible for the political government of India. Thenceforward, whatever were the faults of the Calcutta Government, it was at least free from the temptation to make the administration of an Empire subservient to the dividends of a commercial Company. If it was exacting, its exactions were at least made for the purpose of maintaining a Government and not an Agency—

a Government, too, which was infinitely superior to any other which it overthrew in India.

But nothing made or could make any difference in our dealings with the Rulers of Oude. Acquisitions of territory were now no longer inexpedient; and they were accordingly accepted from time to time in liquidation of arrears. But attention was soon called to considerations which had been before neglected—considerations arising out of the condition of the people and country of Oude. Lord Cornwallis, Sir John Shore, and Lord Wellesley were successively shocked and scandalized by the evidence which they saw of devastation and consequent decay. The consciousness of our own responsibility for that maladministration which was maintained by our bayonets, soon determined the character of our remonstrances. These gradually assumed the tone of rebuke, and then of warning. Lord Wellesley declared in 1799, without reserve or circumlocution, that the grand object to be kept in view was "the acquisition by the Company of the exclusive authority, civil and military, over the dominions of Oude." But, unfortunately, he was contented, in 1801, with a measure far short of that which was required to meet the necessities of the case. A new "treaty" was imposed upon the Nawab, the only effective part of which was the clause which annexed to the dominions of the Company, in lieu of subsidy, a large portion of the territories of Oude. But the remainder of those territories were recommitted to the Government of the Nawab, under the guaranteed protection of the British arms "against foreign or domestic enemies." No other security for its better government was exacted than an engagement that the Nawab "would always advise with, and act in conformity to the counsel of, the officers" of the East India Company in the administration of his country.

Of course the promised amendment never came. For more than half-a-century one of the fairest Provinces of India was subjected to this cruel experiment. Each Ruler seemed weaker and more debauched than the last. One of these was allowed by our Government in 1819 to assume the title of King; but every successive Governor-General had to repeat the same remonstrances and threats. Lord William Bentinck in 1831 was especially emphatic, and addressed a written warning to the King, that unless he reformed his rule, he would be reduced, like the Princes of the Deccan, the Carnatic, and Tanjore, to the condition of a "Pensioner of State." In 1837 Lord Auckland imposed a new "treaty" on the King of Oude, which narrated in its preamble that "inattention to the first duty of a Sovereign on the part of several successive Rulers of Oude has been continued and notorious, and has even exposed the British Government to the reproach of imperfectly fulfilling its obligations towards the Oude people." It was, therefore, provided that the government of the country, in whole or in part, might at any time be assumed by us, any surplus revenue being accounted for to the King. This treaty was, however, disallowed at home; and so far as "treaties" of this nature were concerned, our relations continued to rest on Lord Wellesley's treaty of 1801. At last, in 1847, Lord Hardinge announced that two years' further probation would be given, after which, if there should be no amendment, "His Majesty was aware of the other alternative, and of the consequences." The two years came and went, and two more years, with the same result. But till towards the close of Lord Dalhousie's rule our hands were full, and there was no time to determine on the course to be pursued with Oude. In 1851 the Resident had reported that "His Majesty continues to show the same utter disregard of the sufferings of the many millions subject to his rule. He associates with none but women, singers, and eunuchs."

And so matters continued until, in November 1854, Lord Dalhousie, being urged by the Home Government to take up the long-pending question, determined to confer the appointment of Resident of Lucknow on Colonel

Outram. This appointment was a sufficient guarantee for the spirit in which it was made, for the history of our Indian Services has no nobler name. Thoroughly acquainted with the native character, and holding it a first duty to treat it with consideration always, Outram was the man above every other who might be trusted to give a wise and just opinion on our conflicting duties to the native people and to the native Government. He was instructed to report on the condition of both. Four months' residence in Oude was enough to enable Outram to make his report. The country was a prey to perpetual civil war, and civil war of a most cruel and barbarous kind. The number of persons killed or murdered exceeded two thousand annually. But murder was the least destructive of the many inflictions which completed the misery of the people. Whole towns and villages were frequently burnt, and whole crops destroyed. Sometimes the wives and children of the cultivators were driven off in hundreds, and those of them who escaped death from cold and hunger were sold into slavery.* Such wholesale destruction was not casual or accidental: it formed a regular item in the statistics of crime. The average number of "villages burnt or plundered," for each of the seven years which had elapsed since Lord Hardinge's warning, is stated by Outram at upwards of seventy-eight. The King continued sunk in that gross debauchery which is characteristic of Mohammedan Monarchies when their military virtue has become extinct. Outram did not shrink from the conclusion on which his opinion had been asked. The "extreme measures" threatened by Lord Hardinge could not, consistently with our duty, be longer delayed :—

> In pronouncing an opinion so injurious to the Reigning Family of Oude, I have performed (said Outram) what is indeed to myself a very painful duty; for I have ever advocated the maintenance of the

* See Outram's Report in the Oude Papers, p. 35.

few remaining native States in India so long as they retain any principle of vitality, and we *can uphold them consistently with our duty as the Paramount Power in India* and in accordance with our treaty pledges. It is, therefore, peculiarly distressing to me to find that in continuing to uphold the Sovereign power of this effete and incapable dynasty, we do so at the cost of 5,000,000 of people, on whose behalf we are bound to secure—what the Oude Government is solemnly pledged to maintain—such a system of government as shall be conducive to their prosperity and calculated to secure their lives and property.

The proceedings and discussions which followed the receipt of Outram's report at Calcutta and in England, afford an excellent example of the working of the Anglo-Indian Government when called into action in all its branches, on a great question of Imperial policy. The popular impression which ascribes the annexation of Oude to the special policy of Lord Dalhousie, shows how difficult it is to get that working followed or understood. It is a remarkable fact that of all the Authorities who constituted, or were connected with, the Government of India, Lord Dalhousie took the most restricted view, if not of what we had a right, at least of what it was expedient to do. In the elaborate Minute in which he recorded his opinion, he not only deprecated annexation, but he deprecated even the direct or forcible assumption of the Government of Oude. The distinction between seizing the Government, and annexing the country, may appear a strange one. It is a distinction which must puzzle those who imagine that our relations with the native States of India can be judged by the rules of Grotius and Vattel. But to officers trained in the traditions of the East India Company the distinction was familiar, and appeared to be one of immense importance. They had been accustomed to see Kingdom after Kingdom, and Province after Province, conquered and handed over to their rule. But the ugly word "annexation" had been never used. In the ancient Capitals, where they ruled supreme, they had been accustomed also to see preserved the old Royal and Princely names. In the attempts which have been lately made to connect the mutiny of the Native Army with the "Policy of Annexation," and specially with the annexation of Oude, we sometimes hear of eminent servants of the Company who had always opposed the measure. But when we examine what these officers have really said, we generally find that what they deprecated was not the seizure of Kingly power, but the suppression of the Kingly name. Sir Henry Lawrence is a good example. The contributions of this officer to the "Calcutta Review" have been republished since his death, with a preface by Mr. Kaye. In this preface we are told that "the reader will perceive how consistently opposed was Sir H. Lawrence to what is called the Annexation Policy. He warmly advocated, on grounds alike of justice and expediency, the maintenance of the Native States. A different statement has been made, very ignorantly and very unjustly, on this point." A writer so well informed as Mr. Kaye need not have thus held on by the skirts of a popular delusion. The course which Sir H. Lawrence favoured in respect to Oude, by whatever name it may be called, is plain enough. It is a course which, if submitted to the "Law Officers of the Crown" as a question of International Law, would probably receive from those authorities some name harsher than annexation. The notion that the Rulers of Oude had any Sovereign rights, on account of which we were bound not to interfere with their authority, is scouted by Sir Henry Lawrence with indignation. "Is the fairest Province of India," he exclaims, "always to be harried and rack-rented for the benefit of one Family, or rather to support in idle luxury one member of one Family? Forbid it, Justice—forbid it, Mercy! . . . In every Eastern Court the Sovereign is everything or nothing. The King of Oude has given unequivocal proof that he is of the second class; there can, therefore, be no sort of injustice in confirming his own decree against himself, and setting him aside. He should be treated with respect, but restricted to his palace and its precincts." And this was the course recommended by Sir H. Lawrence not only in the case of Oude, but systematically as a policy applicable to all dependent States. He says of Native Chiefs generally, that they are "mere children in mind, and as children they should be treated." Again: "After a certain career of vice or contumacy, the offender should be set aside, and replaced by the nearest-of-kin who gives better promise."* These passages imply that the British Government has absolute power, not only over the administration, but over the succession to the throne of Native States.

Sir Wm. Sleeman is another example. The Editor of this officer's posthumous work tells us in his preface that Sleeman "constantly maintains the advisability of frontier Kingdoms under native Sovereigns, that the people themselves might observe the contrast, to the advantage of the Hon. Company, of the wise and equitable administration of its rule compared with the oppressive and cruel despotism of their own Princes." Happily, there seems to be no evidence in Sleeman's letters that he ever entertained an opinion at once so weak and so wicked. So far from desiring to keep the people of Oude under a cruel Government from this selfish motive or from any other, Sir W. Sleeman urgently pressed on Lord Dalhousie the duty of relieving them from it. In one letter he says, "Lucknow affairs are now in a state to require the assumption of the entire management of the country." In another letter he says, "The present King ought not certainly to reign. What the people want and most earnestly pray for is, that our Government should take upon itself the responsibility of governing them well and permanently."

These recommendations are in perfect harmony with all the traditions in which the servants of the Company had been born and bred. The course to which they pointed

* Essays, Military and Political, by Sir H. Lawrence, p. 191.

was the course so long familiar in the previous history of India; it was to assume the whole government ourselves, and reduce the native Royal Family to the condition of the puppets who bore the titles of Nawab of Bengal and Nawab of the Carnatic. It is needless to say that this is annexation without the avowal of the name. The question of leaving the King his empty title might be a question of policy, but it could be no question of principle or of right. A delusive form could not alter or modify the substantial character of the act.

There is, indeed, one distinction between annexation and the course recommended by these officers, on which much stress has been laid by them and by their friends. They approved of the seizure of the Sovereignty by the British Government, and they approved of it mainly as due to the interests of the people and of the country. But they had a strange theory that though the King had no indefeasible title to any part of the Kingly power, he had an indefeasible title to the whole of the Kingly revenues. The position was—not merely that the Royal Family of Oude had a claim to be allowed an ample income (for this was admitted on all hands), but that the whole revenue over and above the costs of administration was absolutely due to the King of Oude: that is to say, it was legitimate to seize the Government in the interests of the people, but it was not legitimate to administer for the benefit of the people the revenues of the State. Surely the first claim on the surplus revenues of a country is the alleviation of those burdens from which the revenue is derived. The assumption on both sides is, that the old Government was bad, and that the new Government would be (at least comparatively) good. Yet it was laid down as an axiom by those officers, as if some principle of morality were involved in it, that the good Government must not touch a rupee of that fund which is the most powerful of all instruments for good in the administration of States, and that the whole of that fund must be handed over to the bad Government, which had been condemned as hopelessly corrupt. The whole surplus was to go where it had gone before—to be spent on the pageants and buffooneries and dancing-girls of Lucknow!

It is a very curious question how such a doctrine as this could ever be held by experienced and able men. One cause is probably to be found in the habit, which was traditional in India, of considering the British Government of that country as the Government of a "Company." We can trace this idea in the language of Sir Henry Lawrence, "Let not a rupee come into the Company's coffers."* There would have been at least some meaning in the doctrine if the surplus revenue of Indian States went to increase the private dividends of a commercial Company. But if this was a delusion, the doctrine founded on it was a delusion also. The same right which entitled us to possess ourselves of supreme power in Oude entitled us equally to possess ourselves of the surplus revenue, for the benefit of the people and of the Government of India.

It is a curious fact that Lord Dalhousie alone had scruples even in respect to any forcible seizure of the Government,—scruples which were not shared by such men as Outram or Henry Lawrence. The veriest formalist must admit our right to do what Lord Dalhousie recommended —which was simply to withdraw our troops, declaring the Treaty of 1801 to be at an end. He was induced to recommend this, because he thought the result would be the same. It was by our troops that the Native Government was maintained. Experience had proved that it could not stand without them. If the troops were withdrawn the Government would fall, or would be compelled to seek for our help again, in which case we could impose our own terms. Lord Dalhousie rested his proposal, however, also on grounds of consideration for the Royal Family of Oude, and partly on an assertion, which, if true, was

* Essays, &c., p. 132.

sufficient to decide the question. "The King's consent," he said, "is indispensable to the transfer of the whole or of any part of his Sovereign authority to the Government of the East India Company. It would not be expedient or right to endeavour to extract this consent by means of menace or compulsion." In this paragraph Lord Dalhousie probably overstated his own opinion. The discussion which followed must have convinced him that it was untenable. Not one of the four members of which the Supreme Council of India was then composed supported the Governor-General in the principle he had thus laid down. It was combated, with special clearness and convincing force, in a most able Minute by Mr. (now Sir) J. P. Grant; a paper which should be read by everyone who desires to understand the merits of this question, not only in itself, but in its relation to the past history of India. The Council were unanimous that the Government of Oude should be permanently assumed by the East India Company. Some were strongly in favour of the direct form, as well as of the substance of annexation; but all were agreed that the King's consent was no necessary part of the transaction, and that our right to impose our own conditions upon him must be claimed and asserted. These opinions were recorded between the 18th June and 22nd August 1855, and were remitted for the decision of the Home Government, with this intimation from the Governor-General: "If you should consider that the experience of eight years will arm me with greater authority for carrying the proposed measure into effect than any Governor-General when first entering on the administration of this Empire is likely to command, I beg permission to assure you that I am ready to undertake the duty."

It has been officially stated that the question was brought before the Cabinet, which was the first Cabinet of Lord Palmerston, and at that time included Lord Canning, who had already been designated as Lord Dalhousie's successor. It is a question, therefore, which, unlike most questions of Indian administration, received the deliberate consideration of the Queen's Government, and the decision of which, more directly than others, rested on their final responsibility. The result was a despatch, nominally from the Court of Directors, but really from the Ministers of the Crown, leaving it to the Governor-General to be guided by circumstances as to the mode of securing the desired result, but indicating strongly an opinion that the proposal of withdrawing our troops from Oude was one founded on too limited an interpretation of our rights, and one which, regarded as an indirect measure of compulsion, might involve the risk of failure. The authority of the Court was, therefore, given to Lord Dalhousie, "to assume authoritatively the powers necessary for good government throughout the country," in any form in which he might find it best that this assumption should be effected.

On the morning after this despatch was received a special Council was summoned by Lord Dalhousie, and an unanimous decision was arrived at on the course to be pursued. In this decision several members of the Council yielded something, but the Governor-General yielded most. "I resolved," he says, "to forego my own preferences, and in dealing with Oude to adopt the more peremptory course which had been advocated by my colleagues, and which was manifestly more acceptable to the Honourable Company." Without prolonging controversy on points of principle, but protesting against the doctrine laid down by Mr. Grant, he yet agreed to a course which was logically defensible on no other principle than that which Mr. Grant maintained. The consent of the King of Oude was to be asked to a new treaty; but it was to be asked with notice that if he did not consent, the only difference would be that he himself would lose all security for the name and pension which would otherwise be guaranteed. The position offered to the King was the position which

Sleeman and Lawrence and Outram had indicated as the only position he had any right to keep. He was to be told that we had determined to assume the government of his country; that if he would give his consent he should be guaranteed in the hereditary title and in an ample hereditary revenue; but that if he did not consent, both his position and his income must rest with the Governor-General and Council for the time being. This was very much a repetition of Lord Wellesley's course in 1800–1. It was a course not only defensible but imperatively required; but it is needless to say that it was consistent with no principle applicable to Independent States; and the attempt to avoid the appearance of force, or the avowal of a right which we were nevertheless asserting, proved to be as fruitless as it was unnecessary. The King of Oude behaved with a dignity which even the most degraded Orientals are not unfrequently able to command in the supreme moments of life. He resolutely refused to sign the instrument of his own humiliation. Persuasion, threats, and remonstrance were all in vain. "Uncovering himself, he placed his turban in the hands of Outram, declaring that now his titles, rank, and position were all gone, it was not for him to sign a treaty, or to enter into any negotiation. He was in the hands of the British Government, which had seated His Majesty's grandfather on the throne, and could at its pleasure consign him to obscurity." Yet the Resident retired, we are told, from the Royal presence "with the usual ceremonies and honours" paid to an Indian Sovereign. On the third day after this scene—being the day fixed as a limit by the instructions of the Resident—the Proclamation went forth by which it was announced "that the Government of the territories of Oude is henceforth vested exclusively and for ever in the Honourable East India Company."

The alleged connection of this measure with subsequent events will come under our review hereafter. Meanwhile, it is enough to say that the annexation of Oude, whether as regards its time, its substance, or its form, was less due to any special policy pursued by Lord Dalhousie than perhaps any other act of his Administration.

Nor need we dwell, in connection with our subject, upon the conquest and retention of the Province of Pegu. This was the result of a war with a foreign Power. The whole preparation of the Expeditionary Force was managed by Lord Dalhousie. It was admirably done, and the war was carried to a rapid and triumphant issue. Just as in the Burmese war of 1826, we had conquered and retained the Provinces of Tenasserim, Arracan, and Assam, so in the war forced on the Indian Government in 1848–9 by the arrogance and obstinacy of the Burmese Court, we conquered and retained the Province of Pegu. It was peopled with a race which was friendly to us; it intervened between possessions which were already ours; and it gave us for the future complete command, whether for the purposes of war or commerce, over the great river-mouths of Burmah. But the circumstances of that conquest have no bearing on our policy towards the native States of Hindostan. Lord Dalhousie's government of this Province has been hardly less successful than his government of the Punjaub. So far as we have yet seen, it is an acquisition which is easily kept, and is well worth keeping; though, like every other of the same kind, it was forced upon us by events which were neither foreseen nor desired.

Of all the great acquisitions of territory, then, which happened during Lord Dalhousie's Government, his supposed policy of annexation must rest mainly upon the opinion he expressed, and the advice he gave, on the comparatively small Principalities of Sattara, of Nagpore, and of Jhansi.

Sattara was a Principality which we had ourselves created. The Family which we placed upon its throne was indeed an old one. It represented the great Hindoo Chief who in the seventeenth century had founded the Mahratta Kingdom of the Deccan. But by the time we came into contact with that formidable race, the family of SEVAJEE had shared the usual fate of Eastern Royalty. Its dominions had passed into the hands of usurpers, and nothing remained to it but lodgings in a prison, and the shadow of an illustrious name. When the British Army under Sir John Malcolm in the Mahratta war of 1818 defeated the Peishwah, captured his person, and annexed his country to the dominions of the Company, it was deemed expedient to bestow a small part of that territory, "sufficient for the maintenance of his family in comfort and dignity," upon the hereditary puppet whom Bajee Rao had kept in prison. This was done in the usual form of a "treaty." The Rajah, having violated the conditions imposed upon him, was deposed in 1839, and his next brother was placed upon the throne. The new Rajah had no family of his own; and this fact, as well as the improbability of his having any, had been specially referred to by the (then) Governor of Bombay, Sir J. R. Carnac, as holding out the prospect of the lapse of the Principality to the Government of India, "unless it should be thought expedient to allow the line of Princes to be continued by the Hindoo custom of adoption—a question which should be left entirely open for consideration when the event occurs." Aware of this, the Rajah, in declining health, applied to the British Government for its sanction to the continuance of his "Raj," through an adopted son. No answer had been received to this request when, on the 5th April 1848, the progress of disease warned the Rajah that he must act on the chance of a favourable reply. In the last hours of life, and almost in the agonies of death, the first child that could be found at hand available for the purpose was brought to the dying Rajah, and formally adopted according to Hindoo rites. Was this act to be recognised as conveying the Principality?

Sir George Clerk, who was then Governor of Bombay, alone, of all the authorities in India, was in favour of allowing the succession of the child. But among the reasons urged by this eminent servant of the Company for the advice he gave there is no trace of several assertions which have since been popularly believed. Sir George Clerk did not deny that adoption with the effect of continuing the Raj required the sanction of the Paramount Power. He did not affirm that this was a mere form, or a matter of course, or that all previous precedent and a uniform rule of practice required us to give it. He had himself given peremptory instructions to our Resident at the Court of the Rajah that he was "to abstain from recognising any adoption by means of which the childless Rajah might desire to perpetuate the Sovereignty, assigning to the Rajah as his reason for withholding consent the absence of the sanction of the British Government." Sir George Clerk did not confound, as so many have done since, the right of adoption as conveying Sovereignty with the right of adoption as conveying property, or as qualifying for the discharge of religious duties. He not only admitted but specially dwelt upon this distinction: "The adoption having taken place according to Hindoo usage, there can be no doubt but that such adopted son is the late Rajah's legal heir, and should succeed to all his personal property. The question, however, remains whether he is entitled to the Sovereignty of the Sattara Rajahs." So far from affirming that the refusal to acknowledge this title would be any violation of an established rule, or the beginning of a new policy, Sir George Clerk admitted that no such rule had been established, and that "our views of practice in India in regard to adoptions to Chiefships have been inconsistent and capricious." Sir George Clerk's great argument was that the "treaty" securing the Principality to "heirs and successors," included heirs by adoption as well as heirs by birth. The Rajah had never himself relied on this claim as one on which he could demand the sanction of the British Government to his adoption. His appeal was not to positive stipulations, but to the motives of policy recorded in the preamble. "His Highness," said the

Resident, Mr. (now Sir Bartle) Frere, "quotes the preamble of the Treaty of 1819, and begs that the same motives which induced the British Government to establish the State in the first instance will now lead them to consent to the adoption of a son as his successor." And not only did he ask for this consent as one which he knew to be requisite for his own purpose, but he relied upon it as a means of defence against the claims of others. Among the broken sentences which escaped from the dying Rajah, his entreaties that the British Government would sanction his adoption alternated with entreaties, equally earnest, that the Government would not sanction another adoption which had been made by his own brother, without its knowledge and permission. If Sir George Clerk's opinion, however, were well founded, it was needless to argue on grounds of policy. Nevertheless, he recorded it as his opinion that, "unquestionably a Native Government, conducted as that of Sattara has lately been, is a source of strength to the British Government." This, however, does not really touch the question which was at issue, even as regarded policy. There is no doubt that the Government of the late Rajah had been a good one. But what security was there that it would be equally good under the adopted child? His horoscope had been duly taken, and the stars had been consulted on the three important points of the boy's capacity for rule, his prospect of long life, and the probability of his having heirs. On all these points the "Josees" had reported favourable answers to the dying Rajah. But the infallibility of these prognostications was at least open to doubt; and Sir George Clerk did not suggest that they afforded any strong ground of confidence for the future. His advice was really founded on the views he entertained as to the interpretation of the treaty.

But the Governor of Bombay could not carry his Council with him. On the first point, which was the main one, his arguments were combated in an able paper by Mr. (now Sir J. P.) Willoughby. The new Governor, Lord Falkland—who succeeded when the question was still pending—adopted, after full consideration, the opinion of the Council; and the Governor-General, in a Minute marked by all his vigour and ability, gave his voice against the continuance of the Principality, both on the ground of right and on the ground of policy. The Court of Directors, by a large majority representing the weight of opinion not less than the weight of numbers, adopted the view of the Governor-General:—

> We are fully satisfied that by the general law and custom of India, a dependent Principality, like that of Sattara, cannot pass to an adopted heir without the consent of the Paramount Power; that we are under no pledge, direct or constructive, to give such consent; and that the general interests committed to our charge are best consulted by withholding it.

It was in the discussion of the Sattara question that Lord Dalhousie recorded his dissent from the doctrine—apparently implied though not directly asserted by Sir George Clerk—that the maintenance of native Governments in the midst of our own dominions was in itself politic and advantageous:—

> There may be conflict of opinion (he says) as to the advantage or propriety of extending our already vast possessions beyond their present limits. No man can deprecate more than I do any extension of the frontiers of our territory which can be avoided, or which may not become indispensably necessary for considerations of our own safety and of the maintenance of the tranquillity of our own Provinces. But I cannot conceive it possible for any one to dispute the policy of taking advantage of every just opportunity which presents itself for consolidating the territories which already belong to us, by taking possession of States which may lapse in the midst of them; for thus getting rid of those petty intervening Principalities which may be made a means of annoyance, but which can never, I venture to think, be a source of strength; for adding to the resources of the public treasury; and for extending the uniform application of our system of government to those whose best interests, we sincerely believe, will be promoted thereby. . . . The Government is bound, in duty as well as in policy, to act on every such occasion with the purest integrity and in the most scrupulous good faith. When even a shadow of doubt can be shown, the claim should be at once abandoned.

This is the nearest approach in any of Lord Dalhousie's writings to the advocacy of a "policy of annexation." But the Minute of Mr. Willoughby clearly showed that in the general principle here announced there was nothing new. The idea that Lord Dalhousie was the first to lay down this principle, or the first to act upon it, is entirely without foundation. This principle, and no other, had governed the action of the Indian Government in every previous case in which the failure of natural heirs had been made the occasion of appropriating petty States, Principalities, or Jagheers. It had been explicitly laid down in very similar terms by the Court of Directors nearly twenty years before. And the occasion on which the Home Government then expressed its opinion on this subject was an occasion which directly raised the question as one of principle, and gave, therefore, to their decision all the more importance. Sir John Malcolm appears to have been the first Indian statesman who advocated the expediency of sanctioning adoptions as a system. Among other reasons, he desired to make them a source of revenue, by levying a duty on the successions thereby permitted. This was in 1828. The proposal gave rise to much discussion, and was finally dissented from by the Court of Directors in 1832. Two years later, in 1834, the Home Government laid down the general principle to be followed in these words: "On the whole, therefore, we are unable to frame any more precise direction for your guidance in such cases than that, wherever it is optional with you to give or withhold your consent to adoptions, that indulgence should be the exception, not the rule, and should never be granted but as a special mark of favour and approbation." This principle had been acted on in repeated instances by successive Governments of India. It had been specially raised and decided in a sense adverse to adoption in the petty States of Colaba and Mandavee, and of many Jagheers in the Deccan and Southern Mahratta country. Even the exceptions prove how entirely erroneous it is to suppose that Lord Dalhousie was in any sense the inaugurator of a new policy on this subject. When the Chief of Sanglee had been permitted to adopt, with a view to succession in the Jagheer, it was specially recorded that he was allowed to do so because his "uniform loyalty and good administration gave him the strongest claims to that indulgence." In 1841 the Government of India had recorded their unanimous opinion on this question very nearly in the same terms in which we have seen it repeated by Lord Dalhousie: "To persevere in the one clear direct course of abandoning no just and honourable accession of territory or revenue, while all existing claims of right are at the same time scrupulously respected."*

But the truth is, that under all the reservations with which it has been usually expressed, and with which it is specially guarded by Lord Dalhousie, it leaves room, after all, for every degree of doubt in respect to its application to individual cases. Accordingly, every instance in which native territory has been absorbed within British dominion in India, must be judged on its own merits. It is important, however, to observe that the general principle thus laid down by Lord Dalhousie has exclusive reference to native Sovereignties, and has no adverse bearing on the policy of maintaining a native aristocracy. The right to convey by adoption all private rights and private property was not called in question in the case of Sattara, but was, on the contrary, declared and admitted. Lord Dalhousie not only admitted the adopted boy to be the Rajah's private heir, but he went out of his way to recommend that a special allowance should be assigned to him by the Government of India. All the arguments, therefore, which have been founded on the cruelty of preventing the completion of a rite sacred among Hindoos, are arguments which have no bearing on the question. There was no attempt to interfere with adoption as a religious rite. It must also be remembered that

* Sattara Papers. March 1849.

wherever a native aristocracy exists, or can be created, founded on possessions or position short of Sovereignty, it may be perpetuated by adoption, without in any way contravening the principle of policy laid down by Lord Dalhousie. In the same Minute in which Mr. Willoughby contested the expediency of allowing the Raj of Sattara to be continued he advocated the encouragement of a native landed aristocracy. There is an immense variety in the feudal tenures of India. Some of them are very bad; others it may be expedient to preserve. But as regards native Governments, Lord Dalhousie had seen enough to know that their vices were systematic and their virtues casual. He knew that the dependent position to which they are reduced by our power in India did not contribute to make them better. Sir Henry Lawrence, who knew them well, has said of them: "If they cannot plunder strangers, they must harry their own people. The rule holds good throughout India. The instances among native States where the cultivator is certain of reaping what he has sown, and of being called on to pay only what has been previously agreed, are most rare."* No severer condemnation of native States has ever been pronounced. Lord Dalhousie could not doubt that a rule of succession, which would increase the chance of long minorities, must double every evil and intensify every source of corruption to which such Governments are exposed.

As regards the special grounds, apart from any general principle of policy, on which Lord Dalhousie deemed it inexpedient to maintain Sattara as a native State, these were clearly explained by him: "The territories lie in the very heart of our own possessions. They are interposed between the two principal military stations in the Presidency of Bombay, and are at least calculated, in the hands of an independent Sovereign, to form an obstacle to safe communication and combined military movement.

* Essays, &c., p. 199.

By incorporating Sattara with our possessions, we should acquire continuity of military communication, and increase to the revenues of the State; we should obtain uniformity of administration in matters of justice and of revenue over a large additional tract; and in my conscience I believe we should ensure to the population of the State a perpetuity of that just and mild government which they have lately enjoyed, but which they will hold by a poor and uncertain tenure indeed if we resolve to continue the Raj, and to deliver it over to the government of a boy brought up in obscurity, selected for adoption almost by chance, and of whose character and qualities nothing whatever was known to the Rajah who adopted him, nothing whatever is known to us." *

Jhansi was a case involving the same principles, and decided in the same sense. The Rajah died in November 1853. He left no child, but on the day before he died, very unexpectedly, he adopted a boy five years old, a distant cousin; and the recognition of this adoption was solicited by his widow, the Ranee. But here, as in every other case of annexation, there were some special circumstances affecting it which have been carefully concealed by the opponents of Lord Dalhousie. Like Sattara, Jhansi had been erected into a Principality by ourselves, and was not one of the old Independent States of India. But, unlike Sattara, Jhansi had already been dealt with by the Government of India on the principle of setting aside unauthorised adoptions, and of giving the succession to whom it would. A certain Chief, who was not before recognised as having an hereditary right, had this right first conferred upon him by the British Government in 1817, as a reward of personal service and fidelity. This Chief was further, for the first time, invested with the title of Rajah in 1832. On the day before he died, in 1835, the Rajah adopted a son. But the boy was not

* Sattara Papers. 1849.

recognised as his successor, being set aside in favour of an uncle. This uncle was the Rajah who died in 1853. It was impossible for him to claim as a right that power of adoption which had been set aside in his own favour. But more than this: not only had the right of adoption in this State been set aside in practice, but it had already been made the subject of formal discussion and formal decision by the Supreme Government, both in India and at home. Jhansi was one of the petty States of Bundelcund. In 1837 Sir Charles Metcalfe, with reference to this very question of the right of succession, had laid down the distinction between these States, "which held by gift from a Sovereign or Paramount Power," and the ancient hereditary Kingdoms of India. "In the case," he said, "of Hindoo Sovereign Princes, I should say that in failure of heirs male of the body, they have a right to adopt to the exclusion of collateral heirs, and that the British Government is bound to acknowledge the adoption, provided it be regular. With respect to Chiefs who merely hold lands or enjoy public revenues under grants such as are issued by a Sovereign to a subject, the power which made the grant is certainly entitled to limit succession according to the limitations of the grant, which in general confirms it to heirs male of the body, and consequently precludes adoption. In such cases, therefore, the power which granted would have the right to resume on failure of heirs male of the body." This doctrine had been accepted by the Supreme Government, and, as we have seen, it had been enforced in practice. On this point, then, as Lord Dalhousie said, "there is no need of, and no room for, argument. The historical facts on record negative the Ranee's assertion conclusively; for the previous Rajah did adopt a boy, but the British Government did not acknowledge the boy as successor, and it nominated another person to be Rajah."

As regarded the *policy* of allowing a child to succeed as Rajah when there was no question of right, the previous experience of the State of Jhansi had not been favourable. Even during the rule of the two previous Rajahs the country had been misgoverned, and the revenues had decayed. We had been obliged to assume the management of affairs, and only after they were retrieved had they been handed back to the native Ruler. What prospect was there of better government under an adopted child and the women of the late Rajah? This question Lord Dalhousie answered by referring to the State of Jaloun, where, in 1832, an adoption had been allowed to carry the succession: "In the course of nine or ten years the lands had been profusely alienated; debts to the amount of more than thirty lacs had been contracted; extensive districts had been mortgaged as security for them; there was neither order nor security in the territory; every village was exposed to the attacks of plunderers; cultivation was deserted; and a country which had been fruitful and prosperous was from day to day becoming desolate." "Warned by these results, I hold," said Lord Dalhousie, "that sound policy combines with duty in urging that the British Government, in the case of Jhansi, should act upon its right, should refuse to recognise the adoption, and should take possession of Jhansi as an escheat."

All the circumstances which determined the Government of India to annex Sattara and Jhansi were present in the case of Nagpore, with the addition of many other circumstances special to itself. Nagpore was a remnant of the powerful State which, under the Rajahs of Berar, had been a principal member of the Mahratta Confederacy. The second Rajah was one of the native Princes whose power was shattered at Assaye. Berar, together with other parts of his dominions, was soon after taken from him. In 1817 the fourth Rajah intrigued against the British Government, attacked the Resident and the British troops, was defeated in action, but was nevertheless allowed to keep his throne. A second treachery, however, brought about his fall, and, flying from the vengeance of the

Governor-General, he spent the rest of his life in exile. The State of Nagpore was then, in 1818, "at the mercy of the British Government, and the Musnud at its disposal." Of its own freewill and pleasure that Government determined still to retain, though in strict dependence on itself, a portion of Nagpore as a Native State. It selected for the Musnud an infant boy, who was son of a daughter of the second Rajah; and during his minority it conducted the administration of the country under the nominal Regency of a widow, who was a clever woman, but really through its own Resident, Sir Richard Jenkins. The ten or twelve years of that minority were a happy time for the people of Nagpore. There is but one testimony as to the excellence of the government they enjoyed. Justice was not sold; the taxes were not oppressive; industry flourished, because it was never capriciously deprived of its reward; and the country is described as having become comparatively a garden. Before the minority of the Rajah came to an end, an attempt was made to secure for the people of Nagpore the continuance of these great benefits. In 1826 the arrangement contemplated for this purpose by the British Government was recorded in the usual form of a "Treaty." The young Rajah was held bound to "pay at all times the utmost attention to such advice as the British Government shall judge it necessary to offer him," and "always to conduct the affairs of his Government by the hands of Ministers in the confidence of the British Government, and responsible to it, as well as to His Highness, in the exercise of their duties in every branch of the administration."* Not content with this stipulation, which virtually left the Rajah no sovereignty at all, it was specially declared that the British Government should "have full power and right to assume and bring under the direct management of its own servants any parts of the territorial possessions of His Highness, or the whole, should the welfare of the country require it."†

* Art. X., Treaty. Berar Papers, 1854, p. 5. † Art. XII., Ibid.

But, as usual in such cases, all was vain. This boy, whom we had gratuitously set upon a Throne in 1818, and surrounded with some of the best and most virtuous servants of the British Government, was the same Rajah who died on the 11th December 1843, at the comparatively early age of 46, after a life in which he had broken down his own health by vice, and in which, by neglect and cruelty and avarice, he had not less effectually destroyed the happiness of his people. If any fault is to be charged against the British Government it is not the fault of refusing to perpetuate this Native State, but the fault of having so long suffered it to exist. The picture which is given us of the Court of the country by the Resident, Mr. Mansel, is terrible indeed: but it has been always a common picture among the Princes of the East. Of the Rajah we are told that "a distaste for business and low habits seem the distinguishing features of his temperament." If he ever thought of the "Treaty" which set him on the Throne, he seems to have candidly confessed it was only "as protecting him in the enjoyment of those pleasures of dancing and singing that he had loved from his boyhood." But this was not the worst. The debaucheries of the Palace could only be fed out of the miseries of the people: "Of late years all the anxiety of the Rajah and of his favourite Ministers has been to feed the privy purse by an annual income of two or more lacs of rupees from nuzzurs, fines, bribes, confiscation of property of deceased estates, the composition of public defaulters, or the sale of their effects, and suchlike sources. The Rajah has been thus led on by his avarice to discard all feeling, and to throw himself into the hands of the most unprincipled of his servants, who plundered the country and put justice up to sale for profits. He has done many cruel acts, and even carried war into the country of his feudal dependents. . . . . All this has aggravated the low tone of his mind: he acts and thinks like a village-chandler. The choicest amusement of the

Rajah is an auction-sale, when some unfortunate widow is ruled not to be entitled to her husband's estate." *

This is the Native Government which Lord Dalhousie has been blamed for refusing gratuitously to perpetuate when, happily, it came to a natural end by the death of a vicious and cruel Ruler without any male heir whatever, and without having either attempted, or even desired, to adopt a child. "The Rajah," said Mr. Mansel, "has left four Ranees, but no son or legitimate daughter; nor has His Highness thought of resorting to adoption to supply a successor to the throne, before or during his last illness, though every opportunity was afforded to and even pressed upon him by myself, during the last two years, to lay open his mind upon such a subject, if he entertained the wish. The silence of the Rajah was thus a deliberate act of his own." Yet Mr. Mansel was one of those who recommended that the British Government should once again go out of its way to create an heir, when none existed either by right of birth or of adoption. He did not attempt to found this recommendation on any claim of right, or of treaty obligation. On the contrary, he declared his opinion, after the most careful consideration of the subject, "that the Rajah possessed no right to transmit his Kingdom but to the heirs male of his body lawfully begotten;" and again, that "the general question of the right of adoption did not appear to him to be involved in the present case." His advice was simply founded on that love for Puppet Kings which affected so many of the old servants of the Company. Another boy, described as "amiable and tractable," was to be set up, by allowing the widows to adopt him: and the same cycle of experiments was to be tried all over again.

Of course there were the same arguments by which the same folly had always been advised before: it was true that the people would prefer to be ruled by us; but,

* Papers relating to the Rajah of Berar, 1854, p. 16.

then, there was a native army and a native "aristocracy," which had lived on the squanderings of the Palace, and these would be disgusted by the cessation of the Raj. As for the people, they might be protected by "securities" taken in their interest; it was not necessary to make the Rajah a real Sovereign; all claims would be amply satisfied by the "grant of the titular Raj to one of the members of the Bhonsla family."*

It is needless to say how such arguments were treated by the vigorous intellect of Lord Dalhousie. He would certainly not have allowed an adoption in this case, even if it had been made—by a Ruler who had systematically violated the condition on which he held his State. But since, as a matter of fact, not even the plea of adoption could be urged in this case, Lord Dalhousie entered into a long and perhaps a needless argument on the petition of the widows. After dealing with the claim set up in favour of the right of widows to adopt, when they had not even been desired or empowered by their husbands to do so; after showing that "there exists no person whatever who, either by virtue of treaty, or by custom of the Bhonsla family, or according to the Hindoo law, or according to the Mahratta interpretation of that law, can rightly claim to be the heir and successor of the Rajah just deceased," he concluded that the "gratuitous alienation of the State of Nagpore, for the second time, in favour of a Mahratta youth, is called for by no obligation of justice or of policy."

As regarded the policy of the annexation, Lord Dalhousie said :—

We set up a Rajah at Nagpore. We afforded him every advantage a Native Prince could command. His boyhood was trained under our own auspices; an able and respected Princess was his guardian and the Regent of the State. For ten years, while he was yet a youth, we governed his country for him. We handed it over to him with an excellent system of administration in full and practised operation, with a disciplined and well-paid Army, with a full treasury, and a contented

* Papers relating to the Rajah of Berar, March 1856, pp. 4–6.

people. Yet, after little more than twenty years, this Prince, descending to the tomb, has left behind him a character whose record is disgraceful to him alike as a sovereign and as a man. So favoured and so aided, he has, nevertheless, lived and died a seller of justice, a drunkard, and a debauchee.

What guarantee can the British Government now find for itself, or offer to the people of Nagpore, that another successor will not imitate and emulate this bad example? And if that should be the case, what justification could the Government of India hereafter plead for having neglected to exercise the power which it possessed to avert for ever from the people of Nagpore so probable and so grievous an evil?

Lastly, Lord Dalhousie pointed out the intimate connection between the general interests of the Empire and that only security for good government which could assure to the people of Nagpore the peaceful enjoyment of the fruits of industry. The Valley of Berar and the adjacent districts were among the best of the cotton-fields of India. It was a matter of justice and humanity to the people of Nagpore, but it was not less a matter of Imperial concern to the British Government, that the fertile territory of this State should no longer be wasted and spoiled by the wanton perpetuation of abominable misrule. On this subject Lord Dalhousie's words have a special interest in the present day :—

Under a wise and just administration the people of Nagpore would materially aid in supplying a want, upon the secure supply of which much of the manufacturing prosperity of England depends. Many items go to make up the sum of that prosperity; but there is perhaps no one item in it all upon which more depends than upon a steady and full supply of the staple article of cotton-wool. The importance of this question is ever pressing itself upon all who are connected with the Administration either of England or of India. My own official course during the last ten years has made me especially sensible of its importance. Before I left England it was urged upon me personally by the Chamber of Commerce at Manchester; and during my administration here the Prime Minister has himself addressed me specially upon the increasing interest with which, year by year, it is watched in England. I need hardly say, then, that my attention has never ceased to be directed to the means of obtaining those cheap and abundant fields of supply, and that ready access to them, which alone can relieve England from almost total dependence upon a foreign Power for the supply of an absolutely indispensable material of her trade.

Under all these circumstances, Lord Dalhousie held that "it was the imperative duty of the Government of India not to revive the Raj of Nagpore under a Mahratta Sovereign, inasmuch as it would thereby perpetuate the obstacles which native rule has been proved to place in the way of a vitally important object, which the essential interest of England required him, if possible, to secure. The decision of the Governor-General was ratified by his Council and by the Government at home, and Nagpore became incorporated with the British Empire of India.

It is worthy of remark, in passing, that by this time the Minute of Lord Dalhousie on the Sattara case had become subject of public discussion in India and in England. The passage already quoted, as containing the broadest assertion of his principle, had been especially made matter of animadversion; and Lord Dalhousie, in pronouncing his decision on the case of Nagpore, took occasion to expose the misrepresentations to which he had been exposed. As these misrepresentations are as common now as they were in 1854, it may be well to quote this passage here:—

I have perceived that in the course of public criticism a far wider interpretation has been given to these words of mine than they were intended, or can be rightly made, to bear. I by no means intended to state, nor did I state, an opinion, that the settled policy of the British Government should be to disallow every succession resting upon adoption, made by a native Prince according to the forms of Hindoo law. The opinion which I gave was restricted wholly to "subordinate States," to those dependent Principalities which, either as the virtual creation of the British Government, or from their former position, stood in such relation to that Government as gave to it the recognised right of a Paramount Power in all questions of the adoption of an heir to the sovereignty of the State. In the case of every such State, I held that sound policy at this day required that the British Government should take advantage of any lapse that might occur, whether it arose from the failure of all heirs whatsoever, or from failure of heirs natural, so that succession could only pass by permission being given for the adoption of an heir. But even in the case of such lapse, I declared that no advantage should be taken of it unless it could be done in accordance with the "most scrupulous observance of good faith."

Such were the principal territorial additions by which the frontiers of British India were carried to the line at which they still remain, and at which, in all human probability, they will continue to remain for many years to come.

Much as these questions occupied Lord Dalhousie's time, the eight years of his Administration were marked by events even more important than conquests and annexations. No man who has represented our rule in India had ever prosecuted with so much vigour the works of peace. In England the great public undertakings on which the progress of society and the increase of wealth depend are the fruit of private enterprise; in India they have hitherto rested almost exclusively with the Government. Everything, therefore, has depended on the estimate placed by the Government on their value and importance. Nothing but a very strong conviction could overcome the difficulties with which every Governor-General was beset. The cost of unexpected but almost continual wars, added to the cost of administration over so vast an Empire, had left the Indian Treasury in a state of chronic deficiency. But Lord Dalhousie knew, and acted on the conviction, that the only hope of restoring the balance must come from increased expenditure of a better and more profitable kind. "The ordinary revenues of the Indian Empire," he observes, "are amply sufficient, and more than sufficient, to meet its ordinary charges; but they are not sufficient to provide for the innumerable gigantic works which are necessary to its due improvement. It is impracticable to effect, and absurd to attempt, the material improvement of a great Empire by an expenditure which shall not exceed the limits of its ordinary annual income." Acting on this principle, Lord Dalhousie took a personal and eager part in the prosecution of public works. The charges on account of public works rose in his time to the unprecedented sum of two-and-a-half millions for one year, and to very nearly three millions (sterling) in another. In the Punjaub large sums were at once set apart for the purpose, and great lines of road surveyed and undertaken under the superintendence of the incomparable Lieutenants to whom the administration of that Province had been intrusted. In the same Province, and under the same agency, the Baree Doab Canal was designed and vigorously prosecuted. The entire length of this canal, with its branches, will be 450 miles. The thirsty lands, through which its waters were to be led, were personally inspected by Lord Dalhousie; and he wrote with enthusiasm to the Court of Directors of the benefits which would be conferred upon the people. In the North-western Provinces the great work of the Ganges Canal was pushed forward with vigour until, in 1854, its main stream was opened for the double purpose of navigation and of irrigation. No financial pressure, no exigencies of war, were suffered to interrupt its progress. Of the magnitude of this work some idea may be formed from the facts stated by Lord Dalhousie—that it extends 525 miles in length; that for purposes of irrigation it is fivefold longer than all the main irrigation lines of Lombardy united; that, as regards navigation, it nearly equals the aggregate length of the four greatest navigable canals in France; that it greatly exceeds all the first-class canals in Holland put together; and that it is greater, by nearly one-third, than the greatest navigation-canal of the United States of America.

The Electric Telegraph was rapidly spread over the whole of India. Within fifteen months it was in operation from Calcutta to Agra, thence to Attock on the Indus, and again from Agra to Bombay and Madras. These lines extended over 3,000 miles. To Lord Dalhousie the people of India owe the establishment in their country of the system of cheap and uniform postage—that boon of inestimable value which has placed the name of Rowland Hill very high among the benefactors of mankind. No happier idea has ever been conceived; none has been worked out in practice with more admirable skill, or received such triumphant recognition in every civilised country of the world. Distance, however great, seems to have no effect on its applicability and success. In India a single letter is conveyed from Peshawur, on the borders of Affghanistan, to the southernmost village of Cape Comorin, or from Debrooghur, in Upper Assam, to Kurrachee, at the mouth of the Indus, for a charge of three farthings!

Last, not least, Lord Dalhousie, in 1853, submitted to the Home Government his views on the general question of Railways in India. His advice was that their formation should be encouraged to the utmost. The Court of Directors were urged not to hesitate to engage in the enterprise upon a scale commensurate to the vast extent of the territories which had been placed under their government, and to the great political and commercial interests which were involved. They were urged to do this, not directly by undertaking the work themselves, but by affording such help—by guarantee or otherwise—as might suffice to attract to India the commercial capital and enterprise of England. This he dwelt upon as an object to be aimed at, apart from and besides all other benefits to be derived from the operation of railways in India. The Government of India had—and would always continue to have—public works of another kind on hand, more than sufficient to occupy all the resources at its command. But even if it had not, it should aim, above all things, at the establishment in India of the same spirit of private enterprise on which had been mainly founded the improvement and civilisation of the Western World:—

One of the greatest drawbacks (wrote Lord Dalhousie to the Directors) to the advance of this country in material prosperity, has been the total dependence upon the Government in which the community has placed itself, and its apparent helplessness to do anything for itself. Until very recently the only regular carrier in the country has been the Government, and no man could make a journey but with the Government establishments, or by the agency of a Government officer. It was but the other day that the Agent of Lloyd's in the Port of Moulmein, where there is a considerable community of European merchants, formally complained that the Government of India did not keep a steamtug, to tow their ships to sea for them. Even in those instances in which something like enterprise has been attempted, by means of joint-stock companies, the effect has been feeble — the results insignificant. For years the steam-companies on the Ganges have complained of the competition of Government steamers. During the last year fully one-half of the Government steamers has been withdrawn; nevertheless one of the two steam-companies has ceased to run. It is so in everything else — no one seems to have activity enough, in connection with a company, even to look after his own interests. I submit that any time and money which the Honourable Court could save by undertaking such works itself, would be well expended in securing the introduction, at this time, of a large amount of English capital and English energy, so as to encourage, by the successful issue which I anticipate for these railway undertakings, a more extensive employment of similar capital and similar efforts hereafter in connection with the products and trade of India.

But Lord Dalhousie contended that the Government should retain such control over the execution of the lines as should secure a due application of the capital expended, and should render impossible the wastefulness and jobbery which had been the ruin of so many railway companies at home. The course which has since been actually adopted is to guarantee a minimum rate of interest on the capital advanced by English companies for the construction of railways in India. One evil of this system is that it tends to prevent any rigid economy in the construction of the works; and it may be questioned whether the Government agency of inspection is sufficient to check extravagant expenditure. Yet without a guarantee it is probable that the requisite capital would not have been forthcoming at all; and although that guarantee of five per cent. is now in operation on a total expenditure of some 43,000,000*l.*, causing for a time a heavy drain on the revenues of the Empire, the vast benefits, direct and indirect, which result to the Government are becoming every day more fruitful and more secure.

The sixth year of Lord Dalhousie's rule ended the lease under which, so often renewed, the "Company" still held the nominal Government of India. Consequently, that curious and complicated system which had arisen from the great Parliamentary contest of 1783–4 came once more to be reconsidered.

It is remarkable how little the changes made by the Act of 1854, or the much greater changes which have been effected since, have altered the essential features of the plan struck out by the genius of Pitt. It can never be too distinctly repeated, because it appears to be very little understood, that the Government he established was the Government of the Crown. The purpose for which the Company was maintained was not to limit Parliament or the Crown in matters of government, but to keep their hands off in matters of commerce and of patronage. Pitt always avowed that his Bill was intended to make the Crown supreme in every question of policy and of government. It was not for doing this that he had denounced the Bill of Mr. Fox, and roused against it the jealous indignation of the English people. Fox's Bill did, indeed, propose to do the same, but it had proposed also to do a great deal more. The "Company" was then a commercial body, holding in monopoly a gigantic trade, possessing from that trade an enormous revenue, and having in its pay a staff of servants proportioned in number and in influence to the imperial magnitude of its concerns. All this, without distinction or difference between what belonged to Commerce and what belonged to Government, was equally placed by Fox's Bill under the control and management of a body nominated by the Crown. There would not have been a Supercargo whom they could not appoint, nor a Clerk whom they could not dismiss. There was no restraint on the extent or character of their patronage. A special clause exempted them from even recording their reasons for appointing strangers to any office in the service of the

Company. The proprietors of the Company were to receive from a branch of the Executive their knowledge of their own "debts and credits"—of the "first cost and charges of their investments outwards and inwards—of their shipping accounts—of the produce of their sales, and of the state of their warehouses at home and abroad."*

All this seems to have been much forgotten. Even such men as Mill the historian have misconceived and misrepresented the essential point on which that great contest turned. Pitt, we are often told, when he came into power, did exactly that for which he had censured Fox, inasmuch as by his invention of the Board of Control he completely subjected the Government of India to the Ministers of the Crown. He did so; and he repeated over and over again that he meant to do so. The Indian Empire was the Empire of the British Sovereign, and its government and administration must be subject to the supreme Executive and supreme Legislature of the State. But within the sphere of patronage and of commerce, Mr. Pitt guarded the independence of the Company as jealously as within the sphere of politics he asserted the supremacy of the Crown.† The only exception which he admitted to the power of the Crown in political affairs had reference to the danger of pecuniary corruption, and it is curious that this exception has been maintained to the present day. The Board of Control could impose no new charge on the revenues of India. But with this exception the Court of Directors became, as regarded the Government of India, nothing more than the Councillors of the Minister who presided in

* Mr. Fox's Bill, clause 14.

† The great Whig orators of that time invariably confounded these two questions together. Mr. Pitt insisted on the essential difference between them. Burke in his speech Jan. 16, 1784, said: "The new Bill vested in the Crown an influence paramount to any that had been created by the first (Mr. Fox's) Bill."

Cannon Row. They might be his trusted Councillors; they might be left to pursue their own traditions; but they might also be thwarted at every turn, and instructions might be put into their mouth which they never saw, or which, if they did see, they disapproved. Thenceforward the "Company" were no longer except in name the governors of India. At home, through the Board of Control always, and through the Secret Committee on special occasions,—in India through the Governor-General, who was almost always an English statesman, and was practically nominated by the Minister of the day, the Government of India was the Government of the Crown. It is a signal instance of the power of mere names and of legal fictions, that in spite of these unquestionable facts, the Company has been accustomed to claim all the merit, and its opponents have been accustomed to charge against it all the faults, of the Government of India. On the whole the accusations have been more idle than the boasts. The servants of the Company have formed a school of administrators in whom the Crown has been wont, and did well, to trust. But in so far as the government of India has been in this sense really the government of the Company, their power and influence has been founded either on superior knowledge, or on traditions which secured the assent and approbation of the Ministers of the Crown.

But the power which resulted from special knowledge and special aptitude resided far more in the officers of the Company who were the actual administrators in India, than in the Directors who were the nominal governors at home. It was, however, a real power, and it assisted in maintaining the position of the Company when some of the original supports of that position had begun to fail. In proportion as the mercantile character of the Company declined, its character as a Government emerged in prominence and importance. At the end of their lease, which expired in 1813, they were deprived of their monopoly in the trade to India: at the end of the next twenty years, they were deprived also of the remaining monopoly in the trade to China. Each of these measures was contested, and the contest on the question of commerce served to postpone any further contest as to the question of their position in the Government of India. For the first time, in 1853, the political question arose unembarrassed by any contest respecting commerce. But there still remained one of the two great reasons on account of which such value had been placed on the political position of the Company as an intermediate body between the Crown and the Government of India. Their commerce was gone; their fleets of noble Indiamen no longer brought home to England the teas and the silks of China. But their patronage still remained. Every office in those great Civil and Military Services by which an Empire had been conquered, and through which it continued to be administered,—from the Councillors, whose salaries were double that of the Prime Minister of England, to the Magistrates and Collectors, who ruled over territories which had been Kingdoms, —every commission in an Army which exceeded the British Army in numbers, and rivalled it in discipline, renown, and in feats of arms,—was still at the disposal of the Directors of the East India Company. Through what other channel this vast patronage could be safely dispensed remained as difficult a problem as in the days of Pitt. Other difficulties, which were purely imaginary, in the way of transferring to the Crown the nominal as well as the real government of India, had grown up out of confusion of thought and ignorance of facts. It had been sedulously taught and sincerely believed that the Company was a screen indispensable to veil the Government of India from the action of party in the English Parliament. The truth is, it had never served this purpose, and it never could. On every occasion on which Indian questions had assumed any important bearing on politics at home, they had been warmly contested in the House of Commons. On one memorable occasion they had determined the policy of England, and changed the fate of Europe. Ever since that period, Parliament had known perfectly well that the Ministers of the Crown were responsible for the government of India. It did not often interfere with their discretion, because it had little knowledge of Indian affairs, and because those affairs had generally no connection with the questions of engrossing interest at home. The comparative immunity of Indian politics from the influence of party-contest arose, not from a legal fiction with which all the leaders of party were perfectly familiar, but from the nature of things—from facts which could not be affected, one way or another, by a mere change of name.

But if the Company had come to be credited with benefits which did not really flow from it, on the other hand there was nothing to show that the part which the Constitution did assign to it had been otherwise than well performed. The Directors of the Company were the Councillors of the Crown in its government of India. No Council newly constituted would have the same weight, or represent the same traditions. The erroneous notions which had arisen respecting the benefits of its action were at least a proof of the reputation it had acquired in this, which was its true capacity. Accordingly the Cabinet of Lord Aberdeen, when called upon to deal with this great question, maintained the Company in its old political position; yet they made some changes, which, though now almost forgotten, were really changes of great significance. The Company were continued as Trustees for the Government of India; but they were no longer continued for a fixed term of years. There were no commercial interests requiring the security which such a tenure had been originally intended to afford; there was no longer any reason why Parliament should not be free at any time either to do without a Council, or to change its form and constitution. Still further to mark the Court of Directors as nothing but a Council, its number was reduced by one-fourth, and of the remaining number—18 instead of 24—one-third was for the first time to be nominated by the Crown.

These were great changes, and all tending in one direction. But the greatest change of all effected in the Act of 1854 was that which attacked the real difficulty on account of which the Company had been so long maintained in its political position. Its patronage of the Civil Service was taken from it, and yet that patronage was not given to the Crown. Whether the scheme of recruiting for the Civil Service by free competition will succeed in maintaining or improving the Civil Service of India, it was at least a method of escaping from the alternative which had always been contemplated with such alarm. It was a step, and a long one, towards the greater change which was so soon to follow.

The one great difficulty which still remained was the patronage of the Army and the union of the two Armies—a difficulty which tradition had exaggerated, but which the Cabinet of Lord Aberdeen did not feel itself under any strong necessity to face; and if it had not been for this, there is reason to believe that the measure, which was at last precipitated by the Great Mutiny of 1857, would have been proposed to Parliament in 1854.

There was another change made by the Act of 1854 which had respect to the constitution of the Government in India. This was an enlargement of the Council of the Governor-General, so as to include representatives of the minor Presidencies and some of the Judges of the Supreme Court. But since, in this as well as in other matters, the provisions of the Act of 1854 have proved to be of short duration, we shall defer, to our review of Lord Canning's Government, a full consideration of the important questions involved in the history and constitution of that body.

Looking back, as we now do, upon the years of Lord Dalhousie's rule through the light of subsequent events, we naturally search for anything in the transactions of the time which can have had any bearing on the condition of the Native Army. But in all that respects its organisation and its discipline the character of that great Force had been determined long before. It cannot be said that during those years any new influence was brought to bear upon it. The fidelity of that Army in the field had never been doubted, and at no period of our Indian history had that fidelity been more severely tried. It has been supposed that the disasters of the Affghan war shook our credit with the Native Powers, but there is no reason to suppose that it can have shaken our credit with the Native Army. The Sepoy bore his full share of our defeat, and his full share, also, in the triumphs by which it was redeemed. In the battles of the Sutlej he was as brave and as faithful as in the days of Clive. Perhaps our dependence upon that fidelity was sometimes only too apparent: for it must always be remembered that the fidelity of the native soldier to his European master is based upon the allegiance which is due from the inferior to the superior mind—from ignorance to knowledge—from weakness to power. Every symptom of weakness, every instance of mismanagement in the British officer, tends to shake the confidence of the Sepoy; and even a moment's doubt on the issue of a contest, such as that which troubled all England and all India at Ferozeshah and Chillianwallah, tends in some degree to shake the pillars of our rule. Still, our victory was at last complete. It was the victory of the Sepoy also; and if the consciousness of his own value was increased, this feeling was most fortunately exhibited rather in arrogance towards the Sikhs than in disaffection to ourselves.

But in looking back to the influences affecting the condition of the Native Army, there is one not to be forgotten, and that is, its mere growth in numbers. The great wars in which we had been so frequently engaged, and the conquests of new territory which had been their almost invariable result, had tended steadily to increase the levies by which alone so vast an Empire could be held. Before the Affghan war in 1838 the total Native Force was under 154,000 men; before the outbreak of the first Sikh war, in 1845, it stood at 240,310. Under the pressure of that war the Native Army was materially augmented by Lord Hardinge. At the end of that campaign it was to some extent reduced, and when the second Sikh war arose, in the time of his successor, it was thought that this reduction had been dangerous and premature. Towards the close of Lord Dalhousie's rule, when all his wars were over, and when the risk at least of internal danger had been reduced to a minimum, the Native Army amounted to upwards of 233,000 men. This includes the Contingents of native Princes, which were officered by Europeans, but does not include the independent levies which those Princes maintained for their own purposes. If this vast Force had been ever regarded in connection with even the possibility of a contest of race against race, it would have seemed, and it would have been, a danger compared with which all other dangers were insignificant. But no such thought ever entered into the minds of Indian statesmen, or of Indian soldiers. They knew that without the Native Army our Empire never could have been acquired, and they knew, too, that without it that Empire could not be maintained for a single year. To doubt its fidelity would have been to doubt our own powers of rule. First and foremost among these, the very type and symbol of all the rest, is the power of subduing the native races to our will, and of yoking them to our military service. When that power is lost the Indian sceptre will have departed from us. It is not surprising, therefore, that we look in vain for any symptom of a fear which would have gone so deep and would have implied so much.

There had been, indeed, in the course of our Indian history, mutinies in the Native Army; but they had been almost always of a local and partial nature—from some one or other of the many causes of discontent which are at times unavoidable in dealing with bodies of armed men. On one occasion, and on one occasion only in the history of India, there had been a mutiny which, as we look back upon it now, seems to have foreshadowed the terrible events of 1857. Two regiments of the Madras Army rose in the dead of night on their European comrades. There had been no warning, and there was no suspicion. The English and the native soldier had been engaged together, not long before, in one of the bloodiest of our Indian wars. They occupied together the conquered country, formed part of the same garrison, and mounted guard on the same ramparts. Suddenly there burst forth on the part of the dark race all the symptoms of inextinguishable hate. Every European that could be found defenceless was murdered in cold blood with true Asiatic treachery. The excuse for this foul deed had been offence on account of some military regulation about the shape of a turban, and the cut of a beard. The alarm in India at the time was great, but it was of short duration. Regiments of the same Native Army were led without fear against the mutineers. They were overpowered; and the guilty regiments were erased for ever from an Army whose standards had been always carried with proud fidelity from the days of Arcot until then. This was indeed a memorable event; and the historians of British India have ever since narrated with horror the story of the mutiny and massacre of Vellore. But half-a-century had passed not only unmarked by any repetition of such deeds, but full of testimony to the courage and faithfulness of the Native Army.

One occasion of partial discontent arose during Lord Dalhousie's rule, and led incidentally to that misunderstanding between the Governor-General and the Commander-in-Chief which ended in Sir Charles Napier's resignation. The native regiments serving in the Punjaub, before it was finally annexed, had enjoyed the additional pay allowed to troops serving beyond the frontier. When the Punjaub became a British Province they were reduced to the same pay as that received by their comrades in other parts of the Indian territory. The mutinous spirit evinced by some corps on this reduction was, however, speedily suppressed by the vigorous and prudent measures taken by Sir Charles Napier and by Sir Colin Campbell. At another period—under the impression, as he says, that the temper of the Army was in a critical state arising out of this question—Sir Charles Napier issued, of his own authority, an order respecting military allowances, which incurred the censure of the Governor-General in Council. It is not necessary here to enter into the personal part of that misunderstanding, on which the decision of the late Duke of Wellington, adverse to the conduct of Sir Charles Napier, may well be accepted as conclusive. It is important to observe, however, that in defending his own course, Napier was naturally disposed to make the most of the danger with which he had been called to deal. Accordingly, in the preface of his work "Indian Misgovernment," we find it broadly stated, "Mutiny with the Sepoys is the most formidable danger menacing our Indian Empire." But mutiny such as he had then in view—discontent on questions of pay or allowances—is a very different thing from disaffection founded on religious fanaticism and antipathy of race. The same work shows not only how little this danger was present to Sir Charles Napier's mind, but how eager he was in proposals which may be taken as the most decisive of all tests of his habitual confidence in the Native Army. If the magnitude of our Empire was a source of danger in augmenting too largely the Native Force, it had involved at least one counterbalancing effect of immense advantage. Large as the Native Army was, it had plenty of work to do. The imperfect organisation with which we administered such vast dominions, resulting from the random manner in which they were acquired, had cast upon the Indian Army an infinite variety of duties which dispersed it into a thousand fragments. Except on the frontiers which were most exposed to attack from without, there was no concentration of native regiments, and even then the extent of frontier often interposed a very long march between the separate corps. To military men, who looked to the efficiency of that Army for the purposes of war, this was a perpetual subject of complaint. And, beyond all doubt, if the danger to be most sedulously guarded against was an external danger, those complaints were just. But if the Army itself contained the elements of a formidable danger, the full occupation of its activity in time of peace, and its wide dispersion, was not an evil but a good. Sir Charles Napier not only had no such danger present to his mind, but scouted it as unworthy of a moment's thought. In the celebrated "Memoir on the Military Defence of India," which he gave in to Lord Dalhousie in November 1849, we find the following curious and instructive passage:—

The most important point next to the location of our troops is now to be considered—viz. the immense enhancement of military discipline, and the perfection at which large masses of troops arrive by being collected in numbers. . . . . *All the moral feelings* of an Army and its physical powers are increased by being assembled in large masses. It was said Lord Hardinge objected to assemble the Indian troops for fear they should conspire. This reason I cannot accede to, and have never met an Indian officer who did accede to it; and few men have had more opportunities of judging the Armies of all three Presidencies than myself. Lord Hardinge only saw the Bengal Army as Governor-General, and for a short time. I have constantly commanded and studied Bengal and Bombay Sepoys for nearly eight years, and could find nothing to fear from them except when illused; and even then they are less dangerous than British troops would be in similar circumstances. There is, it seems to me, no danger in their being massed, but very great danger in their being spread over a country as they are now. By concentrating the Indian Army, its spirit, its devotion, and its powers will all be increased; by dispersion, our safety hangs on the want of combination between two or more of our surrounding enemies, and such a combination is so far from being improbable, that its not yet having taken place is almost miraculous.

This passage is decisive on the confidence placed by Sir Charles Napier in the Native Army, and especially on the absence of any idea in his mind that risk could arise out of the antagonism of religion and of race. It is the more remarkable, as we have reason to know that the reference made to the opinion of Lord Hardinge is a correct one, and that he had expressed, in the strongest terms, his sense of the danger which might arise from the Native Army being massed together. With rare sagacity, he had read in the events of the Sikh war a lesson on this matter which others had failed to see. It was the Khalsa Army, not the Lahore Government, which began the Sikh war. The great Force which Runjeet had brought together, and had disciplined with admirable efficiency for the purposes of war, was an Army whose fierce fanaticism, inflamed by concentration and by the sense of power, had become incapable of control. Lord Hardinge alone, so far as we know, of all those who have been connected with the Government of India, had present to his mind the notion that a similar danger might arise in our own Army, and on that ground was opposed to measures which have been often warmly recommended by military men, and were undoubtedly desirable in a purely military point of view.

It must be remembered, however, that the step recommended by Sir Charles Napier was not actually taken; and it is only as testing the state of opinion in India on this subject that the proposal has any interest now. The question therefore still remains, whether anything was actually done, as to the organisation of the Army, during the period of Lord Dalhousie's Government, which can have had any influence—for the better or for the worse—on subsequent events?

There were two steps taken—one of which, so far as it went, was adverse, and the other of which was highly favourable. The measure which was of adverse influence was an increase of the rank-and-file of the Sepoy regiments from 800 to 1000 men; the measure which was of favourable effect was the encouragement and more extended employment of Irregular and Local corps. As regards the first of these, it was a step taken at the urgent solicitation of Sir Charles Napier, after the second Sikh war; and before Lord Dalhousie left India he left on record his opinion that the Sepoy regiments ought to be again reduced to the former strength of 800 men, which had been the strength recommended by Lord Hardinge. This opinion, however, of the Governor-General had exclusive reference to considerations of economy and of military efficiency, and was not founded on any jealousy or suspicion as to the spirit of the native troops. The other measure to which we have referred was one of far greater importance, and has a much closer bearing on the danger which had so long been gathering, but which had lain so long concealed. The Regular regiments of the Line in the Bengal Army had long been recruited principally in the same country and from the same high caste. They had thus acquired a peculiar character, and carried to the furthest limit compatible with any kind of military obedience the insane prejudices of their "peculiar institution." These had been always treated by the British officers not only with respect, but with some tinge even of that kind of sympathy which infects the mind from the mere force of habitual contact with a prevailing sentiment. The history of the world presents no more strange anomaly than the well-tried and desperate fidelity of the Bengal Sepoy to men whose touch,—nay, whose very shadow was, under certain circumstances, a pollution worse than death. But these prejudices had not interfered with the fidelity of the soldier, and the Bengal Sepoy had never failed to follow our standard against that of his own faith and race. For the first time in the Affghan war, when the Brahmin regiments were carried beyond the Indus,—the sacred boundary of their Holy Land,—a general impression arose that the delusions and prejudices of caste had been found to interfere with the duties of a soldier.* Sir Charles Napier was not the man to treat with patience anything which stood in the way of absolute military obedience. He looked in an Army above all things for those qualities which would enable him to say of it, as Wellington in 1814 could say of the noble Army which he led from Lisbon to Toulouse—that it was "an Army which would go anywhere and do anything." His fine military instincts led him, accordingly, to turn with delight to those Irregular corps which the many warlike races of India are so well able to supply, and whose aptitude for our military service had been already effectively proved on the field of battle. In the following passage, speaking of adopting the Goorka regiments into the Line, Sir Charles Napier touches with characteristic genius on a matter of even deeper import than he knew of at the time:—

> Bravest of native troops, they at the battles of the Sutlej displayed such conspicuous gallantry as to place them for courage on a level with our Europeans; and certainly they have a high military spirit, are fierce in war, of unsurpassed activity, and possess great powers of enduring fatigue. . . . Now when the mutinous spirit arose with our Sepoys, the chief leaders were undoubtedly Brahmins; and Brahmins, having a religious as well as a military character, enjoy an immense influence. All the higher Hindoo castes are imbued with gross superstitions. One goes to the devil if he eats this, another if he eats that; a third will not touch his dinner if the shadow of an infidel passes over it; a fourth will not drink water unless it has been drawn by one of his own caste. Thus their religious principles interfere in many strange ways with their military duties. The men of the 35th Native Infantry lost caste because they did their duty as soldiers at Jellalabad; that is, they

* It is probable that there was some exaggeration on this subject, and that the impression was founded on circumstances comparatively trivial. In 1857 Lord Melville made a speech in the House of Lords, which had considerable effect, from the narrative it contained of a Sepoy regiment having refused, on account of caste prejudices, to work at the trenches at the siege of Mooltan. This story has since been positively contradicted by the officer in command of the accused regiment. Lord Melville probably repeated the story from hearsay evidence.

fought like soldiers, and ate what could be had to sustain their strength for battle. There never was a stronger proof, than the annoyance which this noble regiment is said to have since received from others, of the injury which high caste in a soldier does, and the Brahmin is the worst. Having two commanders to obey, caste and captain, if they are at variance, the last is disobeyed, or obeyed at the cost of conscience and of misery. Military rules sit light on the low-caste man, and as a soldier he is superior. If caste chimes in with duty he is glad of it; if not, he snaps his finger at caste. When it was made known that Brahmins were at the head of the insubordinate men of the 13th and 22nd, and that in the first regiment alone there were no less than 430, the necessity of teaching that race they should no longer dictate to the Sepoys and the Government struck me, and my thoughts at once turned for means to the Goorkas, whose motto was "eat, drink, and be merry." Their tenets are unknown to me: it is said they do not like cow-beef, yet a cow would not be long alive with a hungry Goorka battalion. They mess together these Goorkas, and make few inquiries as to the sex of a beefsteak! These, therefore, were men with which to meet the Brahmins of Bengal, and their bristling prejudices of high-caste. (*Indian Misgovernment*, pp. 39, 40).

Long before this the exigencies of our position had led to the formation of Local and Irregular corps. Indeed, there had been no increase in the number of the regiments of the Line since 1825. Some Local corps had been raised by Sir Charles Napier in Scinde; but the system was largely developed under Lord Dalhousie, especially in the Punjaub, at the suggestion and through the agency of Henry Lawrence. The organisation of the Punjaub Irregular Force was a measure which had a most powerful influence on the events which followed. No less than ten regiments were raised, equipped, and disciplined from the races which we had just subdued. This was exclusive of a large force of Military Police. The whole of these levies were separated from the Bengal Sepoys by important differences of tradition or of race; and when the time of trial came they supplied a force of nearly 20,000 men, on whose fidelity the two Lawrences did not count in vain, and by whose aid their saving work was done.

There is one other measure in respect to the Bengal Army which, though not actually adopted in Lord Dalhousie's time, was strongly recommended by him, and was in course of being adopted when the Great Mutiny afterwards arose. It was a measure bearing very closely, though indirectly, on the jealous and exclusive character of the Bengal Sepoy. When Lord Dalhousie was organising the Expeditionary Force against Burmah, the 38th Regiment of Native Infantry refused to go beyond sea. The oath under which the Native Army was enlisted had been drawn up in 1786, and had been never changed. It bound the Sepoy "to march wherever he was directed, whether within or beyond the Company's territories;" but it had been always held that the word "march" was confined to movement by land, and that the Sepoy was not bound to submit to transport by sea. Six regiments only of the whole Bengal Infantry were enlisted as general-service corps, although the whole Armies of Madras and Bombay were available beyond sea. In the case of all these various regiments no difficulty had ever been found in recruiting for general service, nor did it appear that there was any inferiority in the military character of the recruits—none, at least, which should induce the Government to maintain a distinction so inconvenient to itself. Lord Dalhousie therefore recommended that, in future, all new enlistments for the Infantry of Bengal should be made on the terms of their being general-service corps. The fact that this measure tended to break up the close brotherhood and exclusive caste of the Bengal Army must have rendered it distasteful to the classes and families from which it had been so long recruited. This discontent may possibly have been among the causes predisposing to the events which followed. But if so, it may well be questioned whether it was not a discontent proving that the necessity of the measure was even greater than it was supposed to be.

There was yet another change in the condition of the Native Army which had been arising gradually for many years, and which did not escape the anxious notice of Lord

Dalhousie. Those soldier-statesmen who have been bred in the service of the East India Company, and whose character has so often shed imperishable lustre on the British name, were a race of men drawn from the European officers of the Native Army. As our Empire was extended, the drain upon the Staff of the Army became more and more exhausting, until at last it was apparent that the Sepoy regiments had been to a large extent deprived of the presence and the care of those on whom their discipline and fidelity must in the main depend. This most serious evil had been of long standing, but it was aggravated by the additional demand for officers in the extensive Provinces recently acquired, and in the superintendence of public works. It was not merely on civil and scientific employments that their services had been required, but largely also on the purely military duty of organising and commanding the Irregular and Local corps which had saved the Government from increasing the Regular regiments of the Line. Within a few years the Sikh Local Corps, the Guides, the Punjaub Irregular Force, the Pegu and Nagpore Forces, besides eight regiments of Irregular Cavalry, had all been raised and organised under European officers drawn from the Native Army of the three Presidencies. The Company, in order to secure some measure of attention to regimental duty, had laid down regulations limiting the number of officers who could be withdrawn for detached duty from each regiment. But these regulations had been from the first defective—taking no account of absentees from other causes—and, such as they were, it had been absolutely impossible to adhere to them. To such an extent had this evil gone that, in 1856, no less than 803 officers were detached from the Bengal Army alone, whereas, according to the regulations, the number ought not to have exceeded 540. Lord Dalhousie proposed that measures should be taken, and new regulations laid down, the object of which should be to fix not merely the maximum number which might be withdrawn for special purposes from each regiment, but a minimum number which must be always present with the corps. He proposed further the formation of a Staff Corps, such as has been now actually established. The whole subject was one which seems to have been strongly impressed upon his mind. He said :—

> I feel it to relate to a point which is of infinite importance to the efficiency of the Indian Army, and therefore think it my duty to moot it for most serious and early consideration. The employment of military officers in all capacities—staff, detached, civil, and scientific—which has been so greatly extended of late years, has been very advantageous to the interest of officers, and of great value to the Government in the several departments to which they have been admitted. But, looking at the practice in a military point of view, I regard it with considerable uneasiness, as likely to act injuriously in many ways upon the efficiency, discipline, and military spirit of the Company's Army.

It is impossible to pass from the circumstances affecting at this time the condition and temper of the Native Army, without reference to the fact that the urgent necessities of the Russian war had compelled the Government at home to diminish sensibly the number of European regiments in India—thus disturbing that proportion between the two Armies on which so much depends. It is true that this reduction was intended to be only temporary; but the balance was not in fact restored until the time came when the flower of the British Army was called to India for the recovery of an Empire which had been very nearly lost. Lord Dalhousie saw with regret the necessity for a temporary reduction of the European Force ; but the risk which was actually incurred thereby was not the risk against which he had it in his mind to guard. There was not, indeed, any danger which he considered imminent; but the possibility to which Indian statesmen and Indian soldiers always looked was a combination between two or more of the native Powers which still retained some military strength—such, especially, as Cashmere and Affghanistan on the northern with

Nepaul on the eastern frontier. This was a combination much dwelt upon by Sir Charles Napier in his "Memoir on the Defence of India," and it was one the possibility of which Lord Dalhousie thought ought never to be wholly disregarded. But, besides this or any other specific danger, the past history of India had naturally impressed on every mind a vague but well-founded sense of the variety of contingencies which might involve the Goverment in some unforeseen emergency. This state of things was inseparable from the very nature of our dominion; and, founded on this, it was Lord Dalhousie's strong opinion that the relative strength of European and Native troops ought to be very closely watched from time to time—not, indeed, on any abstract principle of proportion between the two races, but with reference to the actual condition, internal and external, of our dominions. Looking at that condition as it stood towards the close of his administration, he was of opinion that the smallest amount of European Infantry which could be relied upon as fully adequate for the defence of India, and for the preservation of internal tranquillity, was thirty-five battalions, of which not less than nineteen ought to belong to Bengal with its dependent Provinces, nine to Madras, and seven to Bombay. At that time there were in Bengal only sixteen battalions—one having been sent to the Crimea, and two being stationed in Pegu. Of the nineteen battalions Lord Dalhousie was of opinion that not less than ten should be stationed below Umballah, and five below Agra. For it is important to observe, as bearing on the events which followed, that the location of the European troops had undergone a change which proved to be a serious danger. As our frontier receded, the location of the bulk of our small European Army receded also. The vast line of country between Calcutta and Agra was left with only two or three regiments, stationed at points many hundred miles apart. Twenty years before there had been not less than six European regiments in the Lower Provinces between Calcutta and Allahabad. Lord Dalhousie found in the same space only two regiments, and he never was able to increase the number. It had been to meet in some measure the views of the Indian Government on this subject that Sir Charles Wood had proposed, in the Bill of 1853, that the number of Local European troops which the Company were allowed to maintain in India should be raised from a maximum of 12,000 to a maximum of 20,000 men. This provision received the assent of Parliament; and, in pursuance of it, one additional European regiment had been raised for each of the three Presidencies before the end of Lord Dalhousie's rule. But, notwithstanding this provision, the total number of European troops had suffered a gradual diminution from 48,709, at which they stood in 1852, to 45,322, at which they stood when Lord Dalhousie closed his government in India.

It would have been strange if one of the most distinguished disciples of Sir Robert Peel had exercised for eight years supreme power in India without applying to its commercial system some of those principles which had made such advance at home, and which are founded on natural laws of universal application. Accordingly differential duties on foreign ships were abolished, and the coasting trade of India was set entirely free. A duty on the import of raw cotton into the North-Western Provinces was abolished; the frontier customs-duties in the Punjaub were abolished also. In like manner, and for similar reasons, all customs and all export duties on the River Indus were abandoned: and, ultimately, the land-frontier customs were abolished in Scinde, as they had already been abolished in the Punjaub.

The period of Lord Dalhousie's rule is remarkable for the full and final declaration by the Government of India of its intentions on the difficult subject of Native Education. It had been long before that Government recognised the fact that we had any duty to discharge in this matter towards the people of India. And when the duty was recognised a difficulty arose in respect to the manner of performing it which was due to the peculiar character and history of the Indian race. The same question could never have arisen in respect to any of the heathen people who had been brought elsewhere under our dominion. The Indian people had a literature and a civilisation older than our own—a literature dating back to a language which was the great forefather of all the tongues of Europe. What, then, was the education which we were bound to give them? Should it be an education in our literature and our knowledge, saturated as it was with our religion; or should it be an education in their own ancient languages and theology? The traditional feeling of the East India Company was something more than tolerance. It was a dread of even presenting to the eyes or minds of the Indian people any teaching which might cross the traditions of their faith, or which could afford any explanation or profession of our own. Accordingly, the first vague efforts after Native Education which received any recognition from the Government, were efforts to revive the old learning and old philosophy of the East. The attempt was futile—as futile as efforts to revive the Mastodon. What the Indian of our day wanted, whether he were Hindoo or Mahommedan, was some insight into the literature and science which were the life of his own time, and of the vigorous race which were the representative of all knowledge and all power to him. It is strange that any other idea of education should have ever been entertained; yet, previous to 1835, all the establishments for education supported by the Government, with the exception of the Hindoo College at Calcutta, were Oriental in character. The medium of instruction was Oriental; the mode of instruction was Oriental. The whole scope of the instruction was Oriental, designed to conciliate old prejudices and to propagate old ideas. It is due to the Court of Directors to say that before this time they had pointed to instruction in European literature as the kind of education to which our efforts should be directed. At last, in 1835, the late Lord Macaulay, being then Chairman of the Board of Public Instruction in Calcutta, denounced the system which had been pursued with a vigour and eloquence which proved decisive:—

> If (he said) it be the opinion of the Government that the present system ought to remain unchanged, I beg that I may be permitted to retire from the chair. I feel that I could not be of the smallest use there. I feel also that I should be lending my countenance to what I firmly believe to be a mere delusion. I believe that the present system tends not to accelerate the progress of truth, but to delay the natural death of expiring errors. I conceive that we have at present no right to the respectable name of a Board of Public Instruction. We are a Board for wasting public money; for printing books which are of less value than the paper on which they are printed was while it was blank; for giving artificial encouragement to absurd history, absurd metaphysics, absurd physics, absurd theology; for raising up a breed of scholars who find their scholarship an encumbrance and a blemish.

One month after this paper was written, the Governor-General (Lord Wm. Bentinck) in Council issued a Minute, declaring it to be the opinion of the Government that "its great object ought to be the promotion of European literature and science among the natives of India." Still, the efforts of the Government were feeble, reaching for the most part only the upper classes in the Presidency towns. To reach the masses of the people the vernacular languages must be employed as the medium of instruction, and some link established between the Government and the native institutions. Education in this sense received its first great impulse from the hands of Mr. Thomason, in the North-western Provinces, who obtained permission to establish a Government school in every tehsildaree within certain districts. The measure was expressly declared to be experimental; but it was attended with such signal success that, in 1853, Lord Dalhousie very earnestly recommended that the system of vernacular education, which had proved so effectual, should be extended to the whole of the North-western Provinces. Not only was this large measure recommended for immediate adoption, but similar measures were advised for the Lower Provinces of Bengal, and for the Punjaub—with such modifications as their various circumstances might be found to require.

While these and other proposals for the extension of vernacular education were still before the Home Government, the Court of Directors addressed to the Government of India their Education Despatch, dated July 1854. It contained a scheme of education for all India far wider and more comprehensive than the Local Government had suggested. Lord Dalhousie very truly says of this despatch—which India owes to Sir Charles Wood, who was then President of the Board of Control—that "It left nothing to be desired, if, indeed, it did not authorise and direct that more should be done than is within our present grasp." In directing the establishment of vernacular schools throughout the districts, of Government colleges of a higher grade, and of a university in each of the three Presidencies,—above all, in establishing the principle of grants-in-aid to all institutions which are open to inspection and give a good education,—this despatch lays the foundation of a system capable of indefinite extension, and to a great extent solves the "religious difficulty" in the same way in which it has been solved in England.

The Government of India had from the first established liberty of conscience, with one strange exception. Converts to Mahommedanism had always been protected—because our courts administered both Hindoo and Mahommedan law; and when a native passed from under the one code he came under the protection of the other. But when a Hindoo embraced Christianity he was left liable to loss of property, in addition to the many other sacrifices against which no law could secure him. Lord Dalhousie's Government abolished this strange and discreditable anomaly. It did so not without some resistance;

and the records of the Parliamentary Committees which sat in 1853, on Indian affairs, prove that there were not wanting among our public men some whose ideas of toleration did not embrace the case of a Christian convert. "I hate a man who changes his religion," is a sentiment which once escaped from the lips of a very liberal politician; and it is one which is perhaps more often entertained than honestly avowed.

The Government of India is an immense subject, and the eight years of Lord Dalhousie's rule was a time of intense activity. Of the infinite variety of subjects which press on the mind of a Governor-General who really does his work, it is possible to touch, in a memoir such as this, only on a very few; and of these few it is necessary to dismiss in a single line questions which were the burden of long and exhausting hours. Lord Dalhousie was an indefatigable worker. From the most distant parts of the dominions which he governed, all his Lieutenants were sure of immediate attention to their demands, and a speedy answer to their despatches. For the most part the men chosen for the post of Governor-General of India have not been men likely to attain the highest office of all in politics at home. But Lord Dalhousie was one of these: he had large views, a rapid intellect, indefatigable industry, admirable habits of business, great self-reliance. He was a vigorous writer, and had the faculty of ready speech. Conscious of his own powers, and of the position he had secured in Parliament, he knew the sacrifice he made in accepting even that "Imperial appointment"* which is the greatest office England has to give, except the government of herself. In its noble but laborious duties he worked without ceasing to the last. When he sailed from Calcutta he left behind him in India, and when he reached home he found in England, the universal impression due to a long and splendid administration. That impression has been for a time obscured by the

* Speech of Lord Dalhousie at Edinburgh, 1847.

occurrence of calamities sudden and terrible indeed. The popular mind, never very steady under the impulse of such events, is all the more easily shaken when very deep interest is joined to very imperfect knowledge. During the two years, or more, when every fifth-rate writer and speaker thought it necessary to have his say against something which he called "Lord Dalhousie's policy," Lord Dalhousie himself maintained a silence which must have been painful, but which was supported by a proud sense of what was due both to others and to himself. He could not well have spoken except in his place in Parliament; and in that place he never appeared again. He felt, and he expressed the feeling, that a time which was a time of intense anxiety to all, and of agony to not a few, was no time even to think of any injustice suffered by himself. There was, after all, nothing to answer which could not be answered by a simple reference to official records of the past. To "Lord Dalhousie's policy" in the Punjaub—to the men he chose—to the Forces he organised—to the people he conciliated—we owe in a very large degree the salvation of India. If it had been possible to carry into effect at once the policy he recommended in respect to the number and distribution of European troops in the Lower Provinces, it is not too much to say that there would have been no massacre of Cawnpore, and no abandonment of Lucknow. We have seen how largely his policy in other matters has been misrepresented and misunderstood. Further evidences of this, on yet other questions, will come before us when we deal with the rule of his successor. Meanwhile, this review of an eventful time will justify the expression of a firm belief that, when the records of our Empire in the East are closed, Lord Dalhousie's administration will be counted with the greatest that have gone before it, and that among the benefactors of the Indian people no name will have a better place than his.

INDIA UNDER LORD CANNING.

"ALL IS WELL IN OUDE!"—such was the announcement, just received by telegraph from Lucknow, which Lord Dalhousie placed in Lord Canning's hands, as the first and the best greeting he could receive on landing.

In announcing this, Lord Dalhousie felt that he was announcing the consummation of a policy which was even more Lord Canning's than his own. Of all his predecessors in the great office which he was then assuming, Lord Canning alone had shared in the responsibility of the Government of India before he touched its shores. He had been a member of the Cabinet to whose final decision the question of Oude had been specially referred. That Cabinet had not only decided on the general course to be pursued, but, in respect to the measures required for carrying their policy into effect, they had announced through the Court of Directors that they were prepared to cover with their own responsibility the doubts and scruples which had embarrassed Lord Dalhousie. Care had been taken that this should be understood by the King of Oude. The Resident expressly told him that "the assumption of the Government of Oude had been ordered by the Court of Directors, with the unanimous consent of Her Majesty's Ministers, of whom the future Governor-General was one; and that Lord Dalhousie had been directed to carry this policy into execution prior to his departure from India." * Little more than two months had elapsed since the orders of the Court had been received. Those orders were delivered to Lord Dalhousie at midnight on the 2nd of January 1856, and the termination of his rule had been fixed for the 1st of March. This was short time for the execution of measures of such importance. By the end of the month the troops of the Company had crossed the Ganges; and on the 7th of February Outram had formally assumed the Government of the country, in the name of the Supreme Government of India.

Lord Canning therefore, when in March 1856 he assumed the Government of India, assumed also the Government of Oude. The work of taking military possession of the country was a work which he found completed. And there was another task, more difficult and more important, which he found completed also. The last weeks of Lord Dalhousie's laborious life in India had been devoted to organising the Government of the new Province, choosing the men who were to conduct it, and laying down the principles on which its people were to be ruled. Lord Canning continued to administer the system which he thus found established. Like so much else which Lord Dalhousie did, the instructions issued for the Government of Oude have generally been spoken of in terms betraying entire ignorance of what these instructions were. Oude was to be ruled as nearly as possible as the North-western Provinces and as the Punjaub had been ruled. Scrupulous respect for all existing rights, whatever those rights might on inquiry be found to be; protection to the cultivator of the soil from farmers of the revenue, who had been the curse of Oude; assessments light, and as equal as they

* Oude Papers, p. 288; Letter from Major-General Outram to the King. Feb. 1, 1856.

could be made; a rapid administration of justice unencumbered with dilatory and expensive forms—these were the leading principles which Outram was to observe in the first summary Settlement of the Province. The essential idea of these instructions was, that our dealings with the people of Oude were to be founded on their own ancient customs, whatever these might be. It was Lord Dalhousie's object "to improve and consolidate the popular institutions of the country, by maintaining the village coparcenaries, and adapting our proceedings to the predilections of the people and the local laws to which they were accustomed." Nor is it true, as has been often said, that any violent course was contemplated in respect to those who were called "Talookdars" in Oude. The rapine habitually exercised by this class had been among the most desperate oppressions of the people. The reports of Sleeman, of Outram, and of Lawrence describe in terrible detail the miseries they had inflicted. But though Lord Dalhousie desired that this class should be thoroughly restrained, and that the Government should deal directly with the village zemindars, or with the proprietary coparcenaries wherever these were found to exist, he intimated at the same time that the claims of the Talookdars, or of others who had exercised power under the former system, "should be brought judicially before the Courts competent to investigate and decide upon them."* Outram was further directed to confirm and maintain all grants of rent-free lands given by the former Government, the genuineness of which could be established.

Such was the nature of the system for the Government of Oude which, in course of being rapidly carried into effect, Lord Dalhousie handed over to Lord Canning. "All was well in Oude"—and all continued to be well for the whole of the first year of Lord Canning's rule. No change was made; nor was there any reason to suppose

* Oude Papers, p. 260.

that change was needed. Discontent, of course, there must have been—deep discontent among the predatory Chiefs, who were now for the first time restrained under a just and powerful Government. But the Talookdars of Oude were as helpless under Outram as had been the Sirdars of the Punjaub under Lawrence. There was every ground for the hope and the belief that a system of government which was no experiment, but one which had been well-tried elsewhere with the happiest results, would in a few more years "become the instrument of restoring to affluence and prosperity one of the most fertile regions of the globe." *

Within six months of Lord Canning's arrival his Government was called upon, out of its superabundant strength, to support the policy of England beyond the frontiers of India. An Expeditionary Force was sent to Persia, commanded by the gallant Outram. It is not necessary to discuss here the policy of the Persian war, or to relate the incidents of its short and successful course. One historical interest, however, attaches to the Persian expedition of 1856–7: it was the last of its kind. Parliament was justly jealous of a war conducted by troops over which it had no regular control in the matter of finance; and this Expedition led to the adoption of a clause in the Act 21 & 22 Vict. c. 106, by which it is now unlawful to apply the revenues of India in support of any military operation beyond the frontiers of India, unless with the consent of both Houses of Parliament.

All the signs of peace in which Lord Canning's Government began, continued to surround his course during the whole of the year 1856. There was no danger apparent, and for the best of all reasons,—there was no danger present, except such dangers as, in India, are never out of sight. It is very difficult to make men believe, when a great calamity has occurred, that it has arisen from causes with which they have been long familiar, but of which they

* Lord Dalhousie's Instructions. (Oude Papers, p. 260.)

have taken little notice. Such causes, though perhaps of tremendous power, always seem small causes, and inadequate to the effect. On the other hand, men readily attribute such calamity to any transaction or event, however weak or inefficient, which has attracted their attention much and recently. Everything, at such times, is seen out of its true perspective, and much that is said, accordingly, is the mere utterance of bewilderment, resentment, or alarm. To this class of delusion must be ascribed the vague confused idea, that the Mutiny of the Army of Bengal was in some way due to the annexation of Oude. It is perfectly true that there was an extensive connection between the Sepoy regiments and the population of that country. A large proportion of the men in every regiment of the Army of Bengal were recruited in Oude, and their families resided there. But if this circumstance gave to the Sepoys any very warm affection for the Native Government, or any warm interest in its stability, they must have been a singular exception to all other classes of their countrymen. The theory requires that they should have considered it a privilege to be under the rule of the King of Oude, and a misfortune to be brought under the rule of the Governor General of India. But the fact, as might be expected, was precisely the reverse. It was the special privilege of the Oude Sepoy that he and his family, from the moment of his enlistment, was able to claim, and did habitually claim, the protection of the British Government through its Resident at Lucknow. If, therefore, the Oude Sepoy rebelled because Oude was annexed, he rebelled, not because he thereby lost any privilege himself, but because a privilege, which he very highly valued, was extended to all his countrymen. Human nature is very bad, but it is not quite so perverse as this; and the truth is that, unlikely and unnatural as such a motive would be, even this motive did not really exist. The Oude Sepoy, though entitled to British protection, was not always able to obtain it. His family was living in a country which was a prey to oppressions without limit and without number; and though he was perpetually appealing to the Resident for protection or redress, the Resident was unable to secure it for one out of a hundred of the complaints to which he had to listen; consequently, the Sepoy had a direct interest, second only to that of his less privileged neighbours, in coming effectually under the Government which was already, in theory, his own. Practically he was still subject to the evils suffered by the community to which his family belonged. Consequently, we find that Sir Wm. Sleeman, in a letter to one of the Directors in 1852, specially referred to the interests and wishes of the Sepoys, not as an argument against, but as an additional reason in favour of our possessing ourselves of the Government of Oude. He says:—

> We have at least 40,000 men from Oude in the Armies of the three Presidencies, *all now, rightly or wrongly, cursing the oppressive government under which their families live at their homes.* These families would come under our rule, and spread our good name as widely as they now spread the bad one of their present ruler. Soldiers with a higher sense of military honour and duty to their salt do not exist, I believe, in any country. To have them bound to us by closer ties than they are at present would, of itself, be an important benefit. (*Sleeman's "Journey through Oude,"* vol. ii. p. 379.)

But if it is a delusion to suppose that the interest of the Oude Sepoy lay in preserving the Native Government, it is, if possible, a still greater delusion to suppose that any feeling of religion or of race can have tended in that direction. The people of Oude is, in large proportion, a Hindoo people, and our Sepoys derived from it were in large proportion Sepoys of the Hindoo faith. They were notoriously not only Hindoos, but generally men of the highest castes, and bigoted beyond others in their religion. The Reigning Family of Oude was a Mahommedan family. It represented a Government which was odious in itself; and it represented, besides, a race and a faith from which the natives of Hindostan had suffered conquest and immemorial oppression.

The notion that the Army of Bengal must have been affected by opinions, on the Oude question, which were the opinions of a small section of Anglo-Indian politicians, stands in curious contrast with the notion that the Sepoy regiments cannot have been really affected to any serious extent by a trivial incident affecting the prejudices of caste. The idea that "greased cartridges" can have had really anything to do with the Great Mutiny, is still a favourite subject of ridicule with many. This estimate of the relative importance of the two matters is very natural from our European point of view. It is an optical deception. The annexation of Oude was a very recent event, and a very important one in the history of Anglo-Indian politics. The difficulties connected with it had held successive Governors-General at bay. At the last moment it had divided the members of the Supreme Government of India. A decision so important in the minds of English statesmen must, it is assumed, have equally attracted the attention, and must have equally affected the minds, of native soldiers. On the other hand, caste is a superstition with which we have long been familiar. We had respected it, acknowledged it, almost shared in it. How could any new effect arise from so old and so well-known a cause? It is true, indeed, that the institution of caste had been long familiar to us. But it is hard for any European to measure or understand the nature of its power. If we would see in operation the tremendous force which produced the Great Mutiny of 1857, we must look not to any political measure, however recent or notorious, but to old familiar incidents in the story of our rule in India. Colonel Skinner, founder of the famous Irregular Force called "Skinner's Horse," gives us, for example, the following account of what happened to himself on the 31st January, 1800, when left wounded on the field after an engagement with the Rajah of Ooneara:—

It was about three o'clock in the afternoon when I fell, and I did not regain my senses till sunrise next morning. When I came to myself I soon remembered what had happened, for several other wounded soldiers were lying near me. My pantaloons were the only rag that had been left me, and I crawled under a bush to shelter myself from the sun. Two more of my battalion crept near me—the one a Soobahdar that had his leg shot off below the knee; the other, a Jemedar, had a spear-wound through his body. We were now dying of thirst, but not a soul was to be seen, and in this state we remained the whole day, praying for death. But, alas! night came on, but neither death nor assistance. The moon was full and clear, and about midnight it was very cold. So dreadful did this night appear to me that I swore, if I survived, to have nothing more to do with soldiering—the wounded on all sides crying out for water; the jackals tearing the dead, and coming nearer and nearer to see if we were ready for them: we only kept them off by throwing stones and making noises. Thus passed this long and terrible night. Next morning we spied a man and an old woman, who came to us with a basket and a pot of water; and to every wounded man she gave a piece of bread from the basket and a drink from her waterpot. To us she gave the same, and I thanked heaven and her. But the Soobahdar was a high-caste Rajpoot; and as this woman was a "Chumar" (or of the lowest caste), he would receive neither bread nor water from her. I tried to persuade him to take it, that he might live; but he said that in our state, with but a few more hours to linger, what was a little more or a little less suffering to us? Why should he give up his faith for such an object? No, he preferred to die unpolluted! *

The strength which, against the cravings of failing nature, could resist the double tortures of such temptation must have been strong indeed. The value which a man places in his honour, or a woman in her virtue, or the proudest in his special source of pride;—the pride of race, the pride of theology, the pride of birth;—the tenacity with which the most saintly Christian clings to a true faith and a holy life,—all are concentrated and caricatured in the passion with which a Brahmin guards from pollution the purity of his caste. And yet that pollution may come to him by no conscious act of his own—by accident—or by the design of another. In a moment he may be degraded, defiled, disgraced,—driven from amongst his kindred, and lost in the world to come. When such a fear takes possession of the mind, it becomes insane.

* Military Memoir of Lieut.-Colonel James Skinner, vol. i. p. 178.

Contact with other minds under similar impressions increases tenfold the tendency to panic. Explanations and assurances which would allay the fears of one are repelled by the ignorance or ill-temper of another. Suspicion becomes terror, and terror becomes hatred, until at last a body of men, especially of armed men, under the sway of such passions, is capable of any treachery and ready for any crime.

This is the power which some writers and speakers in this country have regarded as trivial; and which their ignorance of native character has led them to set aside as less capable of explaining the Mutiny of the Bengal Army than plots or conspiracies of which there is no trace whatever, and which, if they had existed, could never have accounted for the curious and terrible phenomena of 1857.

In the month of December 1856, or early in January 1857, a workman (or "classie") of low caste, in the Arsenal at Dum-Dum, near Calcutta, where the school for musketry practice with the new Enfield rifle was then established, asked a Brahmin Sepoy for a drink of water from his "lotah" or water-vessel. The Sepoy refused, saying, "You will defile my lotah by your touch." The classie answered, "You think much of your caste! Wait a little; the Sahib-logue will make you bite cartridges soaked in cow and pork fat! and where will your caste be then?" These words went home: they were repeated by the Brahmin to his comrades—they flew from mouth to mouth, with corroborations invented and believed. In a few days they had spread among all the native regiments in the stations near Calcutta, and were the common topic of whisperings by day and consultations in Brahmin huts by night. It was not till the 21st of January 1857 that this alarm attracted the serious attention of any European officer. On the evening of that day some of the Sepoys, in conversing with Lieutenant Wright, of the Rifle Depôt, told him that the report had already spread through India, and they feared that when they went to their homes their friends would refuse to eat with them. The men seemed to be ashamed to confess the hold which this fear had taken of their own minds, and each Sepoy, very generally disclaiming it for himself, appealed to its prevalence among his kindred or his caste. But though suspicion had begun to work, it had not shaken their confidence in their officers. The men spoke freely of it, and recommended, as a remedy, that they should be allowed to buy for themselves in the bazaars the ingredients for cartridge-grease. On the 22nd of January Lieutenant Wright reported this to the Adjutant of the Depôt, and supported the recommendation of the men. On the following day this report and recommendation reached Major-General (now Sir John) Hearsey, commanding the Presidency Division at Barrackpore, and was immediately forwarded with his support to the Deputy Adjutant-General of the Army at Calcutta. General Hearsey's letter was dated on the 23rd, but it did not reach the Supreme Government till the 26th. Lord Canning did not lose a day. On the 27th the Governor-General in Council not only approved General Hearsey's recommendation, but issued special orders to the Inspector-General of Ordnance that, with the "least possible delay, he was to submit any suggestions for removing the objections raised by the Sepoys"—that "means must be taken to satisfy them that nothing which may interfere with their caste was used"—and that in the meantime the cartridges were to be issued without any grease at all. On the same day, orders to the same effect were sent by telegraph to the most distant stations in India—where alone similar schools of instruction in rifle-practice had been established—to Meerut, Umballah, and Sealkote.*

* Append. to Papers relative to the Mutinies. Inclosure 10 and 11 in No. I., p. 3. I give my reference to this statement, as Lord Derby, in his speech of Dec. 3, 1857, subsequently published by authority, said: "Throughout the whole of this period, from the beginning of February to the 20th March, no single step, as far as I can find, was

In the meantime signs of agitation had appeared in all the regiments stationed at Barrackpore. On the 26th, these corps were paraded by their colonels, and mutual assurances were exchanged between those officers and their men. On the morning of the 28th, the order of the Government, allowing the Sepoys to choose for themselves the grease required for their ammunition, was made known to every regiment in the cantonment. A very curious change now took place in the object of suspicion—showing the morbid and irrational state into which the men's minds were thrown. Satisfied and silenced on the composition of the grease, they transferred their suspicion and alarm to the composition of the new cartridge-paper. General Hearsey met this new phase of the prevailing mania with persevering temper and patience. Full explanations were addressed to the men as to the composition of the paper. A court of inquiry was appointed, on the 4th of February, and the evidence of the highest-caste native officers and men was taken. That evidence was given freely, and in a respectful spirit. It is sad to read it. No glimmer of human reason can be traced. It is very much the sort of evidence that we may suppose might be given by a shying horse, if he could speak, on the cause of his irrational alarms. The poor bewildered Sepoys had been testing and examining the paper by tearing it, by wetting it, by smelling it, by burning it. One of them, Chand Khan by name, told the Court that, "on the evening of the 4th, a piece of the cartridge-paper was dipped in water, and then burnt. When burning, it *made a phizzing noise* and smelt as if there was grease in it!" General Hearsey, intimately acquainted with native character, saw at once the strength and reality of the panic, and reported on the 7th of February, to the Deputy Adjutant-General at Calcutta, that "this foolish idea is now

taken on the part of the Government, either to disabuse the minds of the Sepoys on the subject of these greased cartridges, or to ascertain their probable intentions," &c.

so rooted in the Sepoys, that it would, in his opinion, be both idle and unwise even to attempt its removal." It is very difficult, however, to make up one's mind that men are absolutely inaccessible to reason, and are reduced by abject superstition beneath the level of the beasts that perish. Lord Canning was quite willing to dispense with the new paper, if the old would do. But it was too thick for the new bore and new ammunition, so this expedient failed. He then immediately ordered a scientific examination of the Enfield cartridge-paper, to satisfy, if possible, the Sepoy mind in respect to the composition. It was found, of course, that the paper was entirely free from grease. There was nothing peculiar about it except that it was very thin, light and strong, and was somewhat glazed from the use of "size."

Meanwhile, new and more serious symptoms were appearing. Bad feeling was evidenced by incendiary fires among the military huts of the cantonment. This is a mode of testifying discontent which was not new in the Indian Army. It is not the work of conspirators anxious to conceal some deep design, but of discontented men ashamed or afraid of expressing their discontent in more articulate form. It is a warning; and warnings are not generally given by those who plot. General Hearsey was indefatigable in his endeavours both to re-establish discipline and to conciliate and satisfy the men. On the 9th he paraded the whole Brigade stationed at Barrackpore, and addressed the men in their own language. He explained to them the glazed appearance of the paper, and the necessity for its new and peculiar quality. He explained also the folly of supposing that the Government had any wish to break down their caste, and the still greater absurdity that it contemplated forcing them to embrace Christianity. He farther endeavoured to explain what Europeans understood by conversion,—how it depended on persuasion of the mind, and was incapable of being effected by violence or trickery of any kind. Finally, in a loud voice he asked the men if they understood all he had said. They nodded assent.* Again, as before, the agitation subsided for a time, and the men and the native officers were reported as quite relieved and happy.

So far the careful and conciliatory conduct of General Hearsey and of Lord Canning had met with its reward. And so matters remained till the 26th of February; when, at the neighbouring station of Berhampore, the officer in command of the 19th Native Infantry, having ordered a parade for exercise on the following morning, was astonished by the men refusing to receive the copper caps, which it was the custom in that corps to issue on the previous night. This officer, Colonel Mitchell, had already explained to his regiment all that had been said to their comrades at Barrackpore, and the ammunition which was about to be served out for practice was not the new ammunition at all, but cartridges on the old pattern, left by the last native regiment which had occupied the station. He was naturally astonished at the objections of the men —assembled the native officers, and warned them to tell their companies that continued disobedience would be severely punished. However natural this language was, it differed essentially from the tone which had been taken with similar fears by General Hearsey. Between ten and eleven o'clock at night, Colonel Mitchell was roused by the sound of drums and shouts from the Sepoy lines. On hastening out he met a native officer, who told him that the men had broken open the "bells of arms," and had loaded their muskets. Colonel Mitchell sent instant orders to bring up some Cavalry and Artillery. On their arrival, he marched down to the parade-ground and found the men armed and formed in line. Some of them shouted out to the European officers, "Do not come on, the men will fire."

* It marks Lord Canning's watchfulness and anxiety at this early period, that some delay in reporting to him the result of this address to the men was animadverted on as "most reprehensible." Inclos. 16 in No. 3 Append. to Papers.

The native officers now surrounded the Colonel, begging him not to be violent with the men. Colonel Mitchell then addressed the men in angry language, in which threats of being sent to Burmah, or somewhere beyond sea, were mingled with imperative orders to lay down their arms. The native officers told the Colonel, that so long as the guns and Cavalry were present they could not prevail on the men to lay down their arms, but if these were withdrawn, the men, who were in a panic of being attacked, would at once return to their duty. Colonel Mitchell, at first too violent, was now not firm enough. He withdrew the Cavalry and Artillery. The men laid down their muskets, retired to their huts, and in the morning responded to the bugle calling to parade as if nothing had occurred.

Such was the first act in the Great Indian Mutiny—the first occasion in which the native soldier was hurried into any act of open insubordination—the first, too, in which an English officer had not dealt towards the Sepoy with perfect temper. It is due to Colonel Mitchell to record that he immediately forwarded to General Hearsey, without a word of comment, a petition from his men, stating their case, with some exaggeration, against himself. It is impossible to read this document, or the evidence taken before the Court of Inquiry which followed, without being impressed with the obvious sincerity of the men, and of the uncontrollable terrors and suspicions which had taken possession of their minds. Their Colonel's angry words, and imperative orders to use the cartridges on the following morning, had confirmed their suspicions. "He gave this order so angrily, that we were convinced the cartridges were greased, otherwise he would not have spoken so." The words following describe with simple force all the invariable features of panic among a multitude of men: "Shouts of various kinds were heard; some said there was a fire, others that they were surrounded by Europeans; some said that the guns had arrived, others that the Cavalry had appeared. In the midst of this row the alarm sounded on a drum—then, from fear of their lives, the greater number seized their arms." The men then narrate how they had since been allowed to inspect the cartridges, and how the different kinds of paper still gave rise to suspicions; they conclude thus:—

From that time onwards all duties have been properly carried on; and so shall be. As long as we live we will faithfully obey all orders; wherever in the field of battle we are ordered to go, there shall we be found; therefore, since this is a religious question, from which arose our dread, and as religion is by the order of God the first thing, we petition that as we have done formerly, we may be now also allowed to make up our own cartridges, and we will obey whatever orders may be given to us.

But Lord Canning saw that the great offence committed by the corps, in having had recourse to arms to resist the orders of their Colonel, and in having been prepared to fire on their officers if they had advanced, was an offence which it was impossible to condone. Accordingly, though delaying any formal decision until the Court of Inquiry had established all the facts, Lord Canning, on the 6th of March, sent to Rangoon for a European regiment of infantry, the 84th, which was stationed there. The message was, that the presence of this corps was "urgently" though, probably, only temporarily required. This only reached its destination on the morning of the 13th of March. Within twenty-four hours the regiment was embarked, and under steam for Calcutta. These and other preparations being completed, Lord Canning, in a Minute dated 27th March, recapitulated all the facts, and announced that the 19th Regiment of the Bengal Army was to be disbanded. In the General Orders issued on the same day, the Governor-General said with force and truth:—

Neither the 19th Regiment, nor any regiment in the service of the Government of India, nor any Sepoy, Hindoo or Mussulman, has reason to pretend that the Government has shown, directly or indirectly, a desire to interfere with the religion of its troops. It has been the unvarying rule of the Government of India to treat the religious feelings of all its servants of every creed with careful respect: and to representations or complaints put forward in a dutiful and becoming spirit, whether upon this or upon any other subject, it has never turned a deaf ear.

But the Government of India expects to receive, in return for this treatment, the confidence of those who serve it.

From its soldiers, of every rank and race, it will at all times, and in all cases, enforce obedience. They have sworn to give it, and the Governor-General in Council never ceases to exact it. To no men who prefer complaints with arms in their hands will he ever listen.

In pursuance of this order, the 19th Regiment was marched to Barrackpore, the head-quarters of the Presidency Division, and, in the presence of all the native corps there stationed, was solemnly disbanded by General Hearsey; the main part of two European regiments, the bodyguard of the Governor-General, and two batteries of field artillery being present to enforce the decision of the Government.

So far all was successful: General Hearsey was even cheered by the disbanded men. The Governor-General had been meanwhile indefatigable in taking every possible measure to reassure the native troops on the subject of their fears. He had ordered a change in the drill exercise, whereby cartridges were no longer to be touched by the mouth, but only torn by the hand. But as in a constitution affected by cancer, on removal of the affected part, the disease breaks out at some new point, so this insane suspicion was now every week reappearing in some new form more malignant than before. Only two days previous to the solemn disbandment of the 19th Regiment, a circumstance more ominous than any had occurred on the same spot. A Sepoy of the 34th Native Infantry, who seemed to be drunk or maddened by excitement, had appeared in the lines of the cantonment at Barrackpore armed, and calling on his comrades to follow him "in defence of their religion." Not one of these comrades would step forward to arrest him; and when two European officers came up to do so, and were engaged in a hand-to-hand conflict with the fanatic, they were assaulted by a mob of soldiers from behind, and struck on the head with the butt-ends of muskets. The fight was only ended when the gallant Hearsey himself rode up with his own hand to arrest the mutineer, who, seeing himself likely to be overpowered, fired his musket into his own breast.

A new difficulty arose to Lord Canning out of the result of the court-martial which was held on this affair. One Sepoy, and one Sepoy only, had come to the assistance of the two officers who were wounded by the mutineer: this Sepoy was a Mahommedan. After a prolonged inquiry into the spirit and temper of the regiment, the Court of Inquiry came to this most embarrassing conclusion—"That the Sikhs and Mussulmans of the 34th Regiment are trustworthy soldiers of the State, but that the Hindoos generally of the corps are not trustworthy." Here was a distinction between creeds as affecting the fidelity of the Native Army never before heard of in the history of India. Could the Governor-General recognise it? If he did, there was no room to doubt what the effect must be on the race and faith which predominated in the Army of Bengal. Lord Canning, with admirable judgment, determined that reward and punishment must be meted out to individuals and companies connected with this mutiny, according to the best evidence of the facts, but that no attempt must be made to "draw a line of distinction between creeds." The opinion of the Court, however, is valuable as indicating the real origin of the Mutiny, before its contagion had widely spread. Contrary to an opinion which still prevails, the revolt was Hindoo in its origin, and not Mahommedan. But Government could make no distinction except upon the ground of individual conduct. Two Sepoys were hanged who happened to be Hindoos, one or two were promoted and rewarded who happened to be Mahommedans, and the whole seven companies which had been present at Barrackpore, and had shown such sympathy with the mutineer, were disbanded.

This last conclusion was not arrived at until the 30th April. The whole of that month had been occupied by courts of inquiry, before which much curious evidence was taken. Meanwhile no new symptoms had appeared. The disbandment of the 19th Regiment on the last day of March, and the capital executions of the Sepoys of the 34th which followed soon after, had seemingly arrested the mania of the Hindoos. The mutiny was suppressed in the Presidency of Bengal. On the 7th of May General Hearsey reported that he no longer required the European troops which had been sent to Barrackpore. It was even thought that the Queen's 84th Regiment might be restored to Pegu. But now at last, after three months' course in the Lower Provinces, the mutinous spirit appeared in Oude. On the 2nd May, the 7th Oude Regiment refused to bite their cartridges on parade; on the 3rd, it was reported to Sir Henry Lawrence as in a very mutinous state. His action was immediate, and cannot be told more shortly than in his own words:—

> Instantly a field battery, a wing of H.M.'s 32nd, one of the 48th and 71st Native Infantry, and of the 7th Cavalry, the 2nd Oude Cavalry, and 4th Oude Infantry, marched against it. The regiment was found perfectly quiet, formed line from the column at the order, and expressed contrition. But when the men saw the guns drawn up against them, half their body broke and fled, throwing down their arms. The disarmed 7th were ordered to return to their lines, and recall the runaways. They were informed that Government would be asked to disband the corps, but that those found faultless might be re-enlisted. The corps had, before the arrival of the troops, given up two prisoners and had offered to give up forty more.

On this news reaching Calcutta it so happened that all the members of the Supreme Government took occasion to express or indicate their opinion on the character of the mutiny, and of the nature of the measures required to meet it. They did not then know that the supreme moment had already come, and that on the very day they wrote their Minutes, the most terrible event in the history of British India had been irrevocably determined. But what they wrote is of infinite interest as a record of Lord Canning's policy. It was the 10th May before Sir Henry Lawrence's report came before the Governor-General. He immediately recorded a Minute that "Sir H. Lawrence had acted with promptitude, and should be supported in the course he had taken." He observed, however, with characteristic fairness and consideration towards the Sepoy, that an explanation should be given why biting of cartridges had been required at all, when the new platoon exercise had dispensed with it. Mr. Dorin, senior Member of Council, thought disbandment an insufficient punishment: "The sooner this epidemic of mutiny is put a stop to the better: mild measures won't do it; a severe example is wanted." Major-General Low, concurring generally with Lord Canning, was disposed to believe in the reality of the dread entertained by the men of loss of caste, and that probably the main body of the regiment did not refuse to bite the cartridges from any disloyalty or disaffection towards the Government. Mr. J. P. Grant concurred in this view, and thought that if more severe punishment were required, it should be limited to a few ringleaders. Mr. Peacock concurred with the Governor-General. These Minutes from his colleagues called forth from Lord Canning a final Minute, in which, after explaining his first more fully, he recorded the following memorable comment on the desire for "severe measures" as a remedy for the distemper which prevailed :—

I also wish to say, that it is my conviction that the measures which have been taken in dealing with the mutineers, HAVE NOT BEEN TOO MILD. I have no doubt that many rank offenders have not had their deserts; but I know no instance in which the punishment of any individual could, with unquestionable justice, have been made more severe; and I am not disposed to distrust the efficacy of the measures, because the present ferment, in running its course over the land, after being checked in the Presidency (of Bengal), has shown itself in Oude and in the North-west. I would meet it everywhere with the same deliberately measured punishments: picking out the leaders, wherever this is possible, for the severest penalties of military law, visiting the common

herd with disbandment, but carefully exempting those whose fidelity, innocence, or perhaps timely repentance, is fully proved.

Up to this time the fears and suspicions of the Sepoys had been treated with entire success. Earnest and unremitting endeavours to satisfy their minds had preceded and accompanied every measure of punishment. Punishment itself had been, as Lord Canning required, strictly measured according to the evidence of individual conduct; and the only kind of punishment administered, except in the case of Sepoys concerned in an armed attack upon the lives of their officers, had been the punishment of dismissal. This was a punishment which the Government had an undoubted right to administer, however genuine might be the dread under which the Sepoys had been moved to disobedience. The very sincerity of their fear, and the inveterate hold it had taken on their minds, was proof that they no longer trusted the Government which employed them. For this the best remedy was to leave its service. But so long as this mistrust had not led them into violence and crime, the "severer measures"—for which there was already a cry, even in the Council Chamber—would probably be unjust, and would certainly be inexpedient. If the same gentleness and the same firmness which guided Lord Canning and Sir Henry Lawrence had guided the conduct of the military tribunals, there is every reason to believe that the danger would have passed away.

Alas! Lord Canning's just and sagacious words, that the mutiny had "not been treated too leniently," received, on the very day on which they were recorded, a terrible and memorable vindication.

On the 24th of April, eighty-five out of the ninety men of the 3rd Light Cavalry stationed at Meerut had refused to receive the cartridges tendered to them. A squad of military recruits having followed their example, were at once summarily dismissed. The Commander-in-Chief, General Anson, ordered the trial of the whole eighty-five troopers by general court-martial, and reproved the artillery officer for having taken the more lenient course of dismissing the recruits, observing that this was a punishment "incommensurate with the offence." The court-martial held under the impulse of this feeling pronounced upon the troopers, on the 8th of May, sentence of ten years' imprisonment with hard labour—a sentence tremendous anywhere, but doubly tremendous in the climate and in the prisons of India. On the following morning this sentence was announced to the whole native troops paraded for the purpose. The prisoners were subjected to the additional degradation of being publicly ironed in front of the brigade. General Hewitt reported with apparent satisfaction, after this operation had been completed, that it was one which "the majority of the prisoners seemed to feel acutely." No doubt they did—and others besides the prisoners felt it acutely, too. On the following evening—the 10th of May—the comrades of the condemned men rose in arms—broke open the jail—liberated the prisoners, who had accumulated to the number of 1,200 men—shot down every European they could meet—and marched off to Delhi. On that memorable night the Great Mutiny of 1857 had entered on its fatal course: all India was in a blaze!

We have thus gone with care through the earliest stages of the Mutiny, up to the moment when it became rebellion, because the facts have never been correctly stated in a connected narrative. They were grossly misstated in a pamphlet, published in the course of 1857, "By One who has served under Sir Charles Napier." We do not know who this officer is. But the only characteristic in which he rivals the great Captain under whom he has served, is the violence of his language and the recklessness of his assertions. This anonymous pamphlet would hardly be worth noticing now, were it not for the fact that, for a time, it completely supplanted the authentic information to be derived from the official papers, and that from it were derived almost all the attacks made upon Lord Canning in the Parliamentary Sessions of 1857–8.* There is still to be traced in the public mind an impression that, though Lord Canning's measures were energetic and wise after the Mutiny had entered on its final stage, they were weak and vacillating at first. How entirely erroneous this impression is, the facts here recorded are an ample proof. It is true, of course, that neither he nor anyone else in India expected the Mutiny to assume the proportions it ultimately did. But most probably it never would have assumed those proportions if his just and considerate conduct had been everywhere pursued. The urgent anxiety he showed to reassure the minds of the Sepoys, and to take every possible measure to satisfy their reason on the object of their alarm, indicated an appreciation of the power and reality of their prejudices which, to this day, is very rare indeed.

On this point it is difficult to estimate the force of the evidence without examining the proceedings of the Courts of Inquiry and the Courts-martial, held during March and April, at Barrackpore. One of the most striking facts elicited then was, the composition of the Sepoy regiments in respect of caste. The 19th Regiment, which was disbanded, contained 559 men of the highest castes—Brahmins and Rajpoots. The 34th Native Infantry—in which the mutinous spirit received the earliest and most serious development, and from which it had spread to the 19th—consisted of 1,089 men, of whom no less than 803 were of the Hindoo faith; and of these, again, no less than 335, including 41 of the native officers, were Brahmins. The consequence of this state of things may easily be supposed. Captain Albert, of the 34th, says, in his evidence, "nearly all the native influence in the regiment is in the hands of Brahmins, who have also a numerical superiority." Captain Drury, another of the

* It went by the name of the "Red Pamphlet," and entirely supplanted for a time the "Blue Books."

officers, informed the court that it was a common saying in the regiment "that the corps was commanded by the Havildar-major, Mooktar Persaud Pandy." And who was he? He was the man in whose hut all the secret conferences were held—conferences in which each man inflamed the superstition of his comrade, by repeating and aggravating all the rumours of the camp—until the whole body was worked up to a frenzy of suspicion, not without whispers of revenge and plans of treason. And why was this man's hut the favourite place of assembly? "I went," said one of the Sepoys, "because he was a very high Brahmin; all the native officers are in the habit of going to his house and staying there for hours." The reluctance of the men to arrest or shoot the murderous Sepoy, on the 29th of March, is explained as a reluctance "to kill a man of his caste." It is not surprising that a brotherhood so close as this, bound together by a common superstition so irrational, should have been liable to uncontrollable fits of panic and alarm.

This was the root of the Mutiny, and this continued to be its essential character throughout. It was this which gave it its passionate and fitful strength; it was this which constituted its organic weakness. There was no concert continuous or prearranged—there were only spasmodic bursts of sympathy; for it is curious how much such affections of the mind seem to follow the same laws which govern diseases of the body. Contagion under special conditions seemed necessary to the spread of the poison. It ran a rapid and violent course among certain corps which had peculiar relations with each other, whilst others, apparently exposed to precisely similar conditions, remained for a time wholly unaffected. When Sir Henry Lawrence so promptly surrounded and disarmed the mutinous regiment at Lucknow, he led against them corps composed of precisely the same materials; and a single wing of one European regiment was the only alien element in the force which he commanded. There was no regiment in which the mutinous spirit took an aggravated form sooner than the 34th. But a few companies of that corps, which happened to be separated from their comrades at Dum-Dum, were entirely free from it, and addressed the Government deploring the disgrace which had been brought upon their body. The same curious phenomena continued to mark the progress of the Mutiny, and to follow its decline. The thinnest partition of outward circumstances, or of mental association, seemed to prevent contagion, or to repel it. The entire Armies of Bombay and of Madras escaped the plague. On the other hand, regiments which through many trials and abundant opportunity had continued sound, were suddenly attacked by the mania, as by the breath of some poisoned air, and broke out at moments when success was hopeless, and when the frenzy could end in nothing but disgrace and death. The conduct of some of them reminds one of nothing so much as of the "herd that ran violently down a steep place and perished in the sea."

Those only who thoroughly understand this essential character of the Great Mutiny of 1857 can understand the inestimable value of Lord Canning's character and conduct. Panic is a disease which propagates itself. The one thing which, above all others, has power to stop its way, is a strong mind holding firmly its own self-control. In virtue of that power even a single voice, in the midst of a raving crowd, is a voice gifted with command. Still more has it that power when the voice is the voice of one who rules. When the Mutiny first assumed its alarming aspect, the European community in Calcutta rushed to the conclusion that the whole Army was in one vast conspiracy. Signs and wonders, hardly less irrational than those which frightened the Sepoys, were quoted as proving that the whole native population were traitors, and that to trust a musket in any native hand was weakness amounting to infatuation. The same impulse extended to the public in England. It found expression in the most powerful members of the Press. It affected the mind of Parliament. Even Lord Derby spoke with severity of the too-lenient punishments inflicted by Lord Canning, and stigmatised the mere disbanding of mutinous regiments as an "act of madness." All this indicates the breadth and violence of the current against which Lord Canning stood so firmly. If Lord Canning had yielded to these natural impulses of anger and of fear, the Mutiny must have become that which it never was,—a war between race and race, with wounds that could never be healed. It was given to him to resist this temper, with invincible moral courage, and a love of justice which will ever be dear to the memory of India and of England. The complaints and accusations made against him at the time are an immortal monument of his fame. We will take an instance. Throughout the Mutiny Lord Canning persevered in showing his confidence in the native races whenever and wherever he had an opportunity of doing so. The employment of natives in civil office, long urged upon the Government of India, had been increasing during recent years. It is perfectly true that, amongst the natives so employed, there were some instances of treachery during the height of the Mutiny. But Lord Canning did not allow this fact to reverse a course of policy on which so much depends. The European inhabitants of Calcutta, in the petition which they signed for Lord Canning's recall, record it as one of the high crimes and misdemeanors of the Governor-General, "that he had lately sanctioned the appointment of a Mahommedan to be Deputy Commissioner of Patna; and also the appointment of other Mahommedans to places of trust—to the great offence," they are pleased to add, "and discouragement of the Christian population of the Presidency." To this and to some other similar accusations from the same quarter, Lord Canning's reply was: "The Governor-General in Council has felt it an imperative duty to discourage, and as far as possible to repress, that feeling of indiscriminate revenge which would confound the innocent with the guilty, and hold every Mahommedan and Hindoo in India responsible for the crimes committed by a comparatively small number of them." We bow with profound emotion before the memory of a man who could hold this language at such a time!

Lord Canning was right in feeling some confidence that native troops might still be trusted; but he was much more right in showing a far greater confidence than he felt. In that tremulous condition of the native mind, the sight of this confidence, and the expression of it, tended to delay, to mitigate, or prevent the assaults of bad feeling. On this principle, when the 70th Native Infantry, stationed at Barrackpore, petitioned that they might march against the mutineers who had seized on Delhi, Lord Canning lost not a moment in himself proceeding to the cantonment, and addressing to that regiment a speech of acceptance, of encouragement, and of thanks. The petition of the 70th, with the reply made to it, was immediately published as a General Order by the Governor-General in Council.

Wise as this conduct was because of its justice, it was still more wise because of its prudence. Lord Canning did not believe in a conspiracy of the whole Native Army; but if he had believed in it, he could not afford to say so. When the Mutiny began he had, in the whole extent of the Lower Provinces, only about 2,400 European troops. The Native Army within the same limits exceeded 29,000 men. Yet these are the Provinces in which alone the Mutiny never assumed dangerous proportions. At the time when the disaffection began, a single regiment constituted the whole European garrison of Calcutta and of the neighbouring station of Dum-Dum. In like manner one European regiment was all that Sir H. Lawrence had to rely upon, if the Native Army had been treated as under suspicion, in the turbulent Province of Oude. But at the same moment that Lord Canning was showing confidence in the general loyalty of the Native Army he was taking instant precautions against its possible defection. As, in the physical world, there are structures which strike the mind with sudden force as evidences of design, so, in the course of history, there are moments when we see, almost with the eye of sense, the Hand which is guiding it to ordained results. The time of the Indian Mutiny was one of these. Distant and unforeseen events had happened and were happening with nice coincidence precisely at the time which was the right time for saving India. The quarrel with Persia had been brought to an end sooner than was expected, and the whole of Outram's Force was ready to return. Another quarrel with China had arisen, and English regiments were already on the sea, passing within hail of India. Not an hour was lost by the Governor-General in sending up those rockets into the sky which told that the ship was in the midst of breakers. The public spirit of Lord Elgin and the energetic exertions of Lord Elphinstone responded with decisive effect to the Governor-General's appeals. When, on the 3rd of June, Sir John Lawrence telegraphed from the Punjaub to Calcutta, suggesting a series of measures which he thought it absolutely necessary to take, Lord Canning was able to reply that every one of them "had been taken long ago." But there was another part of this message from Sir J. Lawrence which well indicates the dangers over which his tact and energy prevailed. It was true, as Lord Canning told him in reply, that Lawrence was "better off for Europeans than any other part of India." It was also true that a large portion of the native troops in the Punjaub were those Local corps which his illustrious brother and himself had raised, and which were separate in sympathy from the Army of Bengal. Yet Lawrence telegraphed on the 3rd June, not only that "the whole Native Army are ready to break out," but that "unless a blow were soon struck, the Irregulars as a body would follow their example." It would be a great error to suppose that because this last danger was averted it was not a real danger when Lawrence wrote. It was averted by the vigour and address with which the military spirit of the Irregulars was turned into a loyal course. No time was allowed for their minds to become exposed to the dangers of inaction. Lawrence knew that the only way to prevent defection was to act as if he had no fear and no suspicion. Accordingly, his Local Forces were hurled against Delhi as if they had been English troops; and in that memorable siege they showed not only a courage, but a zeal and tenacity of purpose, without which in that terrible climate, and at that terrible season, our small European Force could never have achieved success.

All these facts and all other facts of the Mutiny,—both the things which did happen, and the things which did not happen,—prove beyond doubt that it originated in a real panic on the subject of caste. That panic spread among the close brotherhood of the Bengal regiments, because their constitution specially predisposed them to its influence. But it does not follow that some political agencies may not have been at work to suggest, to aggravate, and to make use of the superstition of the Sepoy. It is certain that the panic began not in Oude, not in Delhi, but in the stations close to Calcutta itself. If we can rely on a statement of General Hearsey, this was no new fact in respect to the influence of Calcutta on the Sepoy mind. He wrote on February 8th: "I moreover consider it necessary to add my conviction that the Sepoys are tampered with by designing villains, when on duty in Fort William and Calcutta, it having been frequently noticed by old military residents at the station that after frequent absences on such detached duty, many of them returned to their lines with strange ideas and unsettled minds." This is not unnatural. Whatever elements of discontent exist in our Indian Empire have their head-quarters in the Presidency towns, where they are aided by a smattering of

European knowledge, and European habits of organisation. Thus, we find allusion to a Brahmin agency or religious Hindoo party called the "Dhurma Sobha," which, after the manner of its kind in other countries, had been angered by enactments of tolerance which were to it intolerable. The British Government had—not too soon—saved Indian widows from a frightful death; and still more recently it had saved them from a wretched life, by allowing them a legal second marriage. It is said, and it is quite possible, that agents of this "religious society" had thought they would frighten the Government from such iniquities by sowing the seeds of suspicion and distrust in the Native Army. It was said, too, that the dethroned King of Oude, or at least some of his ministers, had aided in this work. This is possible too, although there is very scanty evidence of the fact. But so far as the Royal Family of Oude is concerned, the party which opposed the annexation of that country have little reason to quote the Mutiny in support of their opinions. It was their object to keep that Family in Lucknow, as the representative of the House of Timour was kept at Delhi. We know what was the result and effect of this policy. It gave to the mutineers a standard and a name, and the semblance at least of a political object. On a smaller scale it would have been the same in Oude. It was inevitable under any circumstances that, when the Mutiny broke out, advantage should be taken of it by the powerful Chiefs, each with his little army of retainers and his fortress, who had so long preyed on the country, and who under our Government could prey no longer. But this was the consequence not of our dethroning the King (which was his own fault), but of our assuming the government of the country, which on all hands was admitted to be necessary. The keeping him as a puppet at Lucknow, on the old traditional system of "the Company," would have only added an additional element of difficulty, and a convenient centre of intrigue. Oude was the only part of India where the mutiny of the soldiers assumed the character of a popular insurrection; and there it did so, not because the people cared for the King, but because one large portion of the people were the brothers and the friends of the mutinous Sepoys, and because another large portion of the people, namely, the military Chiefs and their retainers, feared above all things the establishment of a powerful Government at Lucknow.

The view here taken of the cause and nature of the Mutiny is confirmed by an authority who, perhaps more than any other man, is able to speak from the best opportunities of knowledge. Of the voluminous writings produced by the Indian Mutiny there is no paper more interesting or instructive than the "Letter from Sir John Lawrence, forwarding to the Governor-General of India the Proceedings on the Trial of the King of Delhi." The result of that trial proved that the Mutiny was simply a mutiny, and not an insurrection; that it originated in no political cause whatever, and was not connected with any previous conspiracy:—

Whatever may have been the King's participation in the events subsequent to the outbreak at Meerut, nothing has transpired on the trial, or on any other occasion, to show that he was engaged in a previous conspiracy to excite a mutiny in the Bengal Army. Indeed, it is Sir J. Lawrence's very decided impression that this mutiny had its origin in the army itself; *that it is not attributable to any external or antecedent conspiracy whatever*, although it was afterwards taken advantage of by disaffected persons to compass their own ends; and that its proximate cause was the cartridge affair, *and nothing else*. Sir J. Lawrence has examined many hundreds of letters on this subject from natives, both soldiers and civilians. He has, moreover, conversed constantly on the matter with natives of all classes; and he is satisfied that the general—indeed, the universal—opinion in this part of India is to the above effect.

On the predisposing influence of caste, and the impossibility of avoiding giving offence to its insane alarms, Sir John's evidence is not less remarkable. It appears that a fear and suspicion of the designs of the Government was of long standing, and that the most ordinary measures of material improvement were as obnoxious to suspicion as the grease on the Enfield ball, or the glaze on the cartridge-paper. A Rajpoot Brahmin Sepoy told Lawrence that "more than five years ago the belief had existed, and had nearly brought on a mutiny, that the caravanserais for travellers, and the supply of depôts erected by Government on the Grand Trunk Road, were said to be devised with the object of destroying caste; and that before long, impure kinds of food would be prepared in them, which the people would be forced to buy and eat."

This is not the place to follow in any detail the events of the war. In outline, at least, they are vividly impressed on the memory of all. Everything depended on the siege of Delhi. It began on the 8th of June, and the city was carried by assault between the 14th and 22nd of September 1857. The head-quarters of the insurrection then centred in Lucknow. The relief of that garrison by Havelock and Outram took place on the 25th of September. But the relieving force under Outram was in its turn besieged. The second relief, and the rescue of the women and children, was effected by Sir Colin Campbell on the 22nd of November; but the final defeat of the rebels was not accomplished till March 1858. The heroic defence of the Alumbagh—the successive reliefs of its garrison—and the final reconquest of Oude, must ever rank among the most memorable series of events in the military history of India. Alas! how few of the leaders whose courage and endurance triumphed in that contest are surviving now! Henry Lawrence was killed early in the siege; Havelock died at the moment when he had achieved success; Sir J. Inglis is also dead; and whilst these sheets are passing through the press, we learn that Sir James Outram is no more.* His generous conduct in yielding to Havelock the command to which his rank and his office entitled him was only consistent with his noble character. The Indian Services may well be proud of Outram. He was the very type of the soldier-statesmen

* April 1863.

of whom they have produced so many and such great examples. And Outram represented the class which he adorned—not as they once were, but as, happily, in later times, they have come to be—men who, to the skill and vigour which first acquired our rule in India, have added the Christian virtues which can alone make that rule a blessing to the world and an honour to ourselves. Fierce in fight, but generous and compassionate in council, Outram loved the natives of India, and he carried their hearts by storm. They loved him as military races love a great soldier, and as subject races love a protector and a friend.

What the Mutiny was in its origin it continued to be throughout its course—a fanatical burst of passion in a corrupted Army, attracting to itself all the scattered elements of villany or of discontent which existed in the country, but nowhere representing a general insurrection of any race or of any religion. Proud as we may be of the small British Force which conquered in so many fights, we have reason to be prouder still of the command we exhibited over the thousand tribes belonging to our vast and varied Empire. There was hardly one of the battles we fought and gained in which we did not depend largely on native troops. The very names borne by the different corps which fought for us in the Mutiny seem to represent the width and the strength of our dominion. When the small brigade which could be formed at Meerut moved out to advance on Delhi, the first important accession of strength which it acquired was the "Sirmooree Battalion of Goorkhas." To this corps was intrusted the very key of our position, and it lost half its numbers in killed and wounded. The ponderous siege-trains wended their laborious way to the same point under the escort of the "Nabha Contingent" and of "Farquhar's Beloochees." There was the "Jheend Horse"—there was the "Cashmere Contingent"—there was the "Mooltanee Horse"—there was the "Kumaon Battalion"—there were "Coke's

Puthan Borderers." On the burning Ridge, from which our little Army maintained the siege, no louder cheers were given than when the "Punjaub Guides" came bounding into camp on the morning of the 9th of June. For whence had they come, and how? From the far frontier of Peshawur—a distance of more than 600 miles—marching at the rate of twenty-seven miles a day, every day for three weeks—at a season when the thermometer was standing at 110° in the shade! Nor did they fight less bravely than they marched. Within a few hours of their arrival they were in fierce and triumphant action with the enemy. The three storming columns which assaulted Delhi numbered together 2,850 men. Of these a clear majority were native soldiers. Of the reserve column, numbering 1,200 men, 950 were natives, and only 250 British. At Lucknow, the defence of the Alumbagh would have been impossible but for the incomparable fidelity of the Sikhs and Hindostanees, who formed a principal part of the slender garrison. When the contest must have seemed to them hopeless, they sacrificed every remaining chance of their own safety—resisting every inducement of corruption, defying every thought of fear. Whatever lessons the Mutiny has left behind it, this at least is not among them—that native troops may not be trusted. At no period of our rule did we trust them more—at none did they better justify our trust. It may confidently be said that our mastery over the native races has received in the war of 1857 a new and splendid illustration.

Such having been the Mutiny in its character, what was it in its effects? On what points connected with the Government of India did it throw any light really new? This is a large question, for there is hardly any matter connected with that Government on which it did not rouse or revive debate. Immense, therefore, as the subject is, we must trace, at least in outline, what the results of the Great Mutiny have been—in India and at home—on the form and on the work of government—on the instruments of our administration, and on its principles.

Of all the changes which resulted from it, probably the least important in itself was that on which all eyes for a time were fixed. "The Government of the Company had broken down!" There never was purer nonsense. The Government of India was not the Government of the Company, and it had not broken down. But the delusion under which a mere legal fiction had been so long spoken of as if it were a reality showed that it was high time that the fiction should be done away. Whatever errors had been committed in the Government of India had been the errors of the Crown—of its responsible Ministers in England or in India. The Company, as a governing body, had been dead for more than seventy years. It had been dead, but not buried. Its skin had been preserved, and set up as if it were still alive. In its name all acts were still done in India; in its voice all orders were still sent out from home. Its real condition was notorious, yet habitually forgotten; —published in repeated Acts of Parliament—confessed and explained by Ministers of State, yet constantly spoken of as if all these enactments were unknown,—as if all these confessions were disbelieved. There never was such an instance of the power of mere names. Some ninety years before, when the agents of the real "Company" had ruled and plundered Bengal under the pretended Government of a Nawab, the scandals of this system had been denounced under the name of a "Double Government." The indignant oratory of Burke had kept fresh its hated memory in some of the noblest passages of English eloquence. All trace of that system, and of its evils, had passed away. The very elements out of which it had been born had ceased to exist long before the birth of the present generation. But the sound of this opprobrious epithet had been carried on by tradition through all changes of time and circumstance, and its virtue as a term of reproach survived when all knowledge of its original meaning had been lost.

Every man who had a grievance, just or unjust, real or supposed, against the Government of India, still babbled against it as a "Double Government." There is a sense, indeed, and an important sense, in which it was true that the "Government of India" was, and must always be, a "double Government." There was the Government in India, and there was the Government in England. But this "doubleness" is a necessity of the case, and remains now very much what it was before. The only other shadow of a meaning which had been left to this expression was the "doubleness" which consisted in the Indian Minister sitting in Cannon Row, and his Council sitting in Leadenhall Street.

But the truth is, that this fiction of "the Company" had become a nuisance from the inveterate misconceptions to which it had given rise. Its mischief was far greater in England than in India. It was a serious obstacle to the right understanding of all Indian questions. As Sir George Cornewall Lewis accurately said, it "threw obscurity on the seat of power." But it did more than this—it weakened the authority of the Government of India. It made the Crown and the Parliament and the people forget their own responsibility, and induced them to cast wrongfully upon others blame which, if it attached to anyone, attached to themselves, either directly or through those who represented their authority and wielded their power. On the other hand, the Court of Directors claimed on behalf of themselves merits which really belonged to the Minister who controlled them,—or to the Governor-General who was practically independent of them,—or to that public opinion which did operate through Parliament, slowly but surely, upon the administration of Indian affairs. It would be difficult to say which was the greatest delusion of the two—the delusion which claimed all that was good for "the Company," or the delusion which condemned the Company for calamities which had not the remotest connection with the structure of the Government.

But the Cabinet of Lord Palmerston was justified to take advantage of the feeling which arose from the events of the Mutiny to get rid of forms which had long been emptied of all their meaning. It was time that the Government of India should assume an aspect and address corresponding to its real nature. This is all that can be said in favour of the change. But it is quite enough. On the other hand, there was nothing of any force to be said against the abandonment of a fiction so mischievous in its effects. It was not requisite to abolish anything which had ever been of the slightest value. There was no virtue in the fact that the Indian Council and the Indian Minister were never brought into personal communication. There was no virtue in the fact that part of that Council was still elected by the holders of India Stock. There was no virtue in the fact that despatches dictated by a Minister of the Crown should profess to come from "the Honourable Court." These features of the existing system it was necessary to remove. But almost everything else might remain precisely as it had been since 1784. In respect to the distribution of power between the Minister and his Council, no change whatever was required. The Court had been, and the Council was still to bé, advisers merely. Much discussion arose, as is usual in such cases, on points of very small importance—the exact numbers of the Council, and the preservation of an elective element. The echo of old cries still lingered in the ears of men; and they talked of numbers being necessary to "independence"—as if the size of a Council could give the semblance of an authority which was excluded by direct provisions of the law. The only consideration of the slightest importance in determining the number of the Council was that it should be large enough to facilitate a convenient subdivision of the business. Lord Palmerston's Government proposed that the number should be eight, all to be nominated by the Crown, but under restriction as to the qualifications of those who were to be eligible. After the change of

Government, and the failure of Lord Ellenborough's famous proposal that certain English towns should elect a portion of the Council, the discussion ended in the number being fixed at fifteen—eight to be nominated by the Crown, and seven to be elected by the Council itself. The weight of this body, as the adviser of the Minister on questions of Indian administration, depends not on its numbers, but on the knowledge and experience of the men who compose it. The old "servants of the Company," who formed so large a part of the Court of Directors, were the only class in which this knowledge and experience could be found: and it is a just tribute to the noble qualities for government which have flourished in our Civil and Military Services of the East, that Parliament has indicated those Services as the principal source from which the Indian Councillors of the Crown shall continue to be drawn.

As regards the administration of affairs in India, no change whatever of principle was required. It is, therefore, more than doubtful whether it was expedient to issue any Proclamation to the People of India—such as that which the Cabinet of Lord Derby issued in the name of the Crown—as if any new authority were for the first time assuming their government. In respect to religious toleration there was nothing to promise, except an adherence to former practice. This is a far safer guide for the expectations of a people than the words of a Proclamation, which are liable to endless misinterpretation. Lord Canning spoke wisely when he said (referring, however, to another case), "I believe that the issue of Proclamations is not the surest or safest mode of influencing the natives of India. The experience of the past year has furnished examples of the ingenuity with which the meaning of such documents can be perverted, or their language misrepresented by the enemies of the State." The Government was not a new one, neither were its principles of administration new. Already the words of the Proclamation are used as an armoury for debate, and are wildly quoted as consistent or inconsistent with the tenor of particular measures. "We do strictly charge and enjoin all those who may be in authority under us, that they abstain from all interference with the religious belief or worship of any of our subjects." Would this have prohibited the abolition of Suttee?—or the measure securing to converts their share of their family posessions?—or the act legalising the marriage of Hindoo widows?—or the support by "grants-in-aid" of missionary schools? There is no end to such questions. The progress of society and the advance of civilisation in India has "interfered with," and must inevitably interfere more and more with, the habits and customs and legal principles of a barbarous religion. But every step in that advance could heretofore be contested only on general principles of justice or of policy. In future they will be contested with reference to the words of a Royal Proclamation which are not capable of definite interpretation. This is a dangerous position for a written promise coming from the Crown. It is like bringing the personal authority of the Sovereign within the circle of political contention. It would have been better to stand on the character which the Government of India had never forfeited, and which it required no new Proclamation to define.

On the very eve of its dissolution as the traditional representative of an independent power in the administration of Indian affairs, the Court of Directors was called upon to deal with an event which seems to gather up within the shortest compass all the difficulties and anomalies connected with the form of government at home, together with perhaps the most formidable of all questions affecting our rule in India. In January 1858 the Army of Sir Colin Campbell was being concentrated for the capture of Lucknow and the final subjugation of Oude. Lord Canning moved from Calcutta to Allahabad to be near the seat of war, and to determine on the course to be pursued for the pacification of the great Province which the Mutiny had temporarily wrested from us. He found it to be as clear in Oude as in the rest of India, that the defeat of our Government would have been the triumph of anarchy. There was the party of the Begum and her son, claiming to represent the Royal Family of Oude; there was the party of a Mahommedan fanatic called the Moulvie; the party of the Nizam, an adventurer without rights or property in the Province; the Sepoys, who sold their services to the highest bidder; and the Talookdars and Zemindars,—all jealous of each other, and ready to devastate and plunder as before. But all these factions had been equally hostile to the British Government. Yet there was one class, at least, for whom we had done much during the single year of our rule, and from which therefore it had been expected—perhaps unreasonably—that we might derive some support. This was the village proprietors—the actual occupiers of the soil. The condition of this class when we took possession of the country had been one of unparalleled depression. Their rights had ceased to exist, or were reduced to a mere shadow. They were completely in the power of the Talookdars, and were subject to every kind of oppression, tyranny, and exaction. We had restored their independence, and founded our Land Settlement mainly on a direct recognition of what we believed to be their old hereditary rights. But, whether from their weakness or from other causes, this class had shown us no favour in our hour of need. In truth, they had fallen again under the subjection from which we had redeemed them, and had joined the ranks of those who had risen in arms against us. Sir James Outram reported that the village communities had fallen too low to enable us to make them, with safety to ourselves, the basis of our Land Settlement in Oude.

Lord Canning came to the conclusion that it would be absolutely necessary to start afresh. The universal character of the insurrection gave the right, and afforded the means, of doing so. It was impossible, indeed, to treat the people of Oude as we treated our own Sepoys, or the revolted subjects of our older Provinces. Lord Canning therefore put aside altogether, in respect to Oude, the punishments of death, imprisonment, and transportation. But he determined to declare that the Government of India held itself free to deal with the land of Oude—disencumbered from engagements which had been considered favourable to the people, but which had failed to secure their gratitude or contentment. Those engagements had been cancelled by rebellion; and he deemed it indispensable that the Government should resume that right over the soil which every Government in India has asserted in its dealings with the people, and which is the basis of all Indian finance. The moment therefore Sir Colin Campbell's army had cleared the city of Lucknow, and the reconquest of the Province was virtually secured, Lord Canning issued the famous Proclamation which rewarded a few faithful Talookdars by a perpetual confirmation of their estates, and declared that with those exceptions, and with the exception of such other persons as might establish similar claims upon the favour of the Government, the "proprietary right in the soil of the Province was confiscated to the British Government, which would dispose of that right in such manner as to it might seem fitting."

Translated into the English language, and interpreted by European ideas in respect to property in the soil, this was undoubtedly a sweeping measure. There was, however, at this time at the head of the Board of Control a Statesman who knew India, and who ought to have known how different are the principles which prevail there, and which have been familiar to the people through all their history. Proprietary right in the soil, or a right which—whether so called or not—is virtually the same, belongs, and has always belonged, to the Government of India. It is only parted with under leases or "settlements" more or less favourable to the Feudatories and to the occupiers of the soil—which leases are constantly revised and altered under a power which is practically a proprietary power. To put an end to the first Settlement made in Oude on the ground of subsequent rebellion was a punishment strictly measured to the offence. It was one which native rulers under similar circumstances had always been in the habit of enforcing. It was one which did not touch the honour of the most sensitive Rajpoot or Brahmin. It was one, finally—the only one—which would enable us to resettle the country under conditions better suited to the ascertained condition of the people. Nevertheless, the prudence of issuing such a Proclamation was fairly open to discussion. Its terms were considered inexpedient by Sir James Outram on the spot, and the Indian Minister had an undoubted right to act upon his opinion in the matter. He was bound, however, to intimate that opinion in a manner consistent with Lord Canning's position, and with the maintenance of his authority in India. But there was one temptation which Lord Ellenborough could not resist. In more respects than one he is, perhaps, the greatest orator in Parliament, and, like other great orators, he will sometimes sacrifice much to the rhythm of a stately sentence. Seizing on the Secret Committee—that strange instrument of Government devised by Mr. Pitt for bringing the will of the Minister to bear at once and secretly on the Government of India—Lord Ellenborough issued against Lord Canning the celebrated despatch which very nearly destroyed the Cabinet of which he was a member. It is easy to understand the pleasure with which ear and hand followed the march of these sounding periods :—

Other conquerors, when they have succeeded in disarming resistance, have excepted a few persons as still deserving of punishment, but have with a generous policy extended their clemency to the great body of the people.

You have acted upon a different principle; you have reserved a few as deserving of special favour, and you have struck, with what they will feel as the severest of punishments, the mass of the inhabitants of the country.

We cannot but think that the precedents from which you have departed will appear to have been conceived in a spirit of wisdom superior to that which appears in the precedent you have made.

Not content with this rebuke to the Governor-General, Lord Ellenborough—he who had struck down the unfortunate Ameers of Scinde and had annexed their country—condemned in no indirect terms the annexation of Oude, misrepresented broadly the grounds on which it had proceeded,* and implied a doubt whether we had any good right to hold the Province. This "secret" despatch was instantly published in England. Whatever were the merits of Lord Canning's Proclamation, this public denunciation of his conduct before all India, in the very crisis of a dangerous insurrection, was—and was felt to be—an outrage. Lord Ellenborough, with a manliness which is never wanting in his conduct, saved his colleagues by sacrificing himself. The Court of Directors, following in the wake of public opinion in England, passed

* As this erroneous statement of Lord Ellenborough is a very common one, it may be as well to specify it here. It is as follows: "We dethroned the King of Oude and took possession of his Kingdom by virtue of a treaty (1801), which had been subsequently modified by another treaty (1837), under which, had it been held in force, the course we adopted could not have been lawfully pursued; but we held that it (the treaty of 1837) was not in force; although the fact of its not having been ratified in England, as regarded the provision on which we rely for our justification, had not been previously made known to the King of Oude." This sentence is not expressed with the clearness usual in Lord Ellenborough's writings. But the assertions it contains are as erroneous as they are confused and contradictory. First,—We did not profess to act under the Treaty of 1801. On the contrary, Lord Dalhousie's first step was to declare that treaty, and all other treaties, abrogated, because the King of Oude had not fulfilled them. Secondly,—It is not true that we "relied for our justification" on any provision of the Treaty of 1837, which was null. Thirdly,—It is not true that we derived advantage from the non-ratification of the Treaty of 1837. On the contrary, Lord Dalhousie would have been delighted to proceed under it, if it had been in force. It gave him all he wanted —a right to seize the government. The King, however, was offered a better position than that treaty would have secured to him.

a vote of confidence in Lord Canning. This may be said to have been the last important political act of "the Company." Once before, they had exerted against the same Statesman the only formidable power which had been left them by Mr. Pitt; and, in spite of the Ministers of the Crown, had recalled the Governor-General, who was by law their "servant," but who had determined too ostentatiously to become their master. The change which deprived the Council of the Indian Minister of this last remnant of original authority was, of course, inevitable. It was a power which never was, and never could be, exerted except under the protection of such an amount of public feeling in England as would find adequate expression in the British Parliament.

Meanwhile Lord Canning pursued his course of policy in Oude with complete success. The Proclamation, probably, had little or no effect; because, practically, it never reached the people until acts had superseded words. They looked to what was done, not to what was said. Within little more than a month after the capture of Lucknow, almost all the large Talookdars of Oude had tendered their allegiance—by letter, by "vakeel," or in person. Our officers had even in some cases to advise them to delay declaring themselves until the armed bodies of our own mutineers had been dispersed. Lord Canning impressed upon his agents that their "dealings with the chief rebels should be as conciliatory as might be consistent with the dignity of the Government." In proportion as the masterly arrangements of Sir Colin Campbell restored our military possession of the Province, no difficulty was found in convincing the people that our "confiscation of the proprietary right in the soil" was perfectly consistent with a resettlement on liberal conditions, according as their conduct might deserve. The principle on which this resettlement proceeded was that indicated by Sir James Outram. The events of the rebellion were assumed as proving that the village communities were too feeble, and too broken by the oppressions to which they had been so long exposed, to enable them to hold that position in Oude which had been given to similar communities in the Punjaub, and in our own North-western Provinces. The alternative was to lean more on the Talookdars as the responsible landholders, and to give a more general and more extended recognition to their position and authority.

It must be remembered that the Land Settlement originally ordered by Lord Dalhousie, and carried into effect during the first year of Lord Canning's Government, was avowedly experimental—to last only for three years, and to give way afterwards to such permanent arrangements as might be found on detailed examination to be most consistent with the real rights of the various parties having different interests in the soil. It was only pending this inquiry that the actual occupiers were to be assumed as having the primary rights which are involved in possession. This Settlement was therefore perfectly consistent with the final recognition of the Talookdars in any capacity or position to which they might be found, after due inquiry, to have a just and reasonable claim. Whilst this first temporary Settlement was going on, Lord Canning did not take any alarm as to its effect upon the people; nor did he admit that the events of 1857, as affecting Oude, were connected with the measures of the Government or the acts of its local officers. On the contrary, he tells us that "the assessment was moderate, and the Settlement on the whole was completed in conformity with the views then generally entertained of sound policy."* But he assumed that the rebellion had furnished new evidence upon that policy—evidence which superseded the necessity of the more elaborate inquiry originally intended. He adopted the opinion that "the maintenance of a territorial aristocracy is an object of so great importance that we may well afford to sacrifice something

* Despatch, November 29th, 1859.

of a system which, whilst it has increased the independence and protected the rights of the cultivators of the soil, and augmented the revenues of the State, has led more or less directly to the extinction or decay of the old nobility of the country." It was in pursuance of this policy that he determined to base the new Land Settlement on the claims of the Talookdars; but to limit their power, and guard it from abuse by such restrictions in their new grants as might protect the rights of the occupiers and cultivators of the soil. It was an express condition in the "Sunnuds" or charters granted to the Talookdars, that "all holding under them should be secured in the possession of all the subordinate rights they formerly enjoyed."

It is evident that the virtue and even the justice of such a system must entirely depend on the force and efficiency given to these restrictions on the power of the Talookdars of Oude. Of Lord Canning's intentions to secure and protect equally all subordinate rights in the soil, there can be no doubt whatever. But, considering all that we know of the manner in which the Talookdars had acquired their power, it is impossible not to have the strongest misgiving of any system which should assume the *status quo* before our annexation of the Province as the basis of the "proprietary rights" which we are to sanction and enforce. A single example will suffice to indicate the amount of injustice which might be inflicted by an indiscriminate support of the claims asserted by Talookdars. One of the most powerful of this order in Oude is a certain Rajah Maun Singh. An account of the rise of this man's family, and of some of his own treacherous and cruel acts, will be found in Sir W. Sleeman's "Journey through Oude." Maun Singh is described as "shrewd, active, and energetic, and as unscrupulous as a man can be. Indeed, the uncle, old Bukhtawar Singh himself, is the only member of the family that was ever troubled with scruples of any kind; for he is the only one whose boyhood was not passed in the society of men in the every-day habit of committing with impunity all kinds of atrocities, cruelties, and outrages. There is, perhaps, no school in the world better adapted for training thoroughbred ruffians (men without any scruple of conscience, sense of honour, or feeling of humanity) than the camp of a revenue-contractor in Oude. It has been the same for the last thirty years that I have known it. All Rajah Bukhtawar Singh's brothers and nephews were bred up in such camps, and are thoroughbred ruffians." * Yet under the Talookdaree Settlement this representative of a "native aristocracy" is said to have been recognised as the owner of upwards of one thousand townlands, embracing some 500 square miles of territory.

It is not, however, a question of mere personal character, but of justice to others, who are, at least, equally entitled to our protection, which renders it absolutely necessary to test the claims of such men as Maun Singh by the strictest enquiry. It is the method by which their territorial power was acquired—not as a matter of history, or in former generations, but in our own time, a very few years ago, and as a consequence of the misrule which we had so long culpably permitted, in suffering such a Native Government to exist. Here is the account which Sir W. Sleeman has given us of the process by which a certain number of villages with their territory have come to be added to the possessions of Maun Singh. They were let in 1817 to Dursun Singh, his father:—

The bestowal of an estate in jagheer, or farm, ought not to interfere with the rights of the proprietors of the lands comprised in it, as the Sovereign transfers merely his own territorial rights, not theirs; but Dursun Singh, before the year 1820, had, by rackrenting, lending on mortgage, and other fraudulent or violent means, deprived all the Syud proprietors of their lands in the other five villages. They were, however, still left in possession of Bhudursa. He pursued the same system, as far as possible, in the other districts which were from time to time

* Sleeman's Journey. Vol. i. pp. 163–4.

placed under him as contractor for the revenue. He had to contract for Sultanpoor and other districts, altogether yielding fifty-nine lacs of rupees a year, in 1827; and it was then that he first bethought himself of securing his family permanently in the possession of the lands he had seized, or might seize upon, by "Cynamahs," or deeds of sale, from the old proprietors. He imposed upon the lands he coveted rates which he knew they could never pay; took all the property of the proprietors for rent, or for the wages of the mounted and foot soldiers, whom he placed over them, or quartered upon their villages, to enforce his demands; seized any neighbouring banker or capitalist whom he could lay hold of, and, by confinement, or harsh treatment, made him stand security for the suffering proprietors for sums they never owed; and when these proprietors were made to appear to be irretrievably involved in debt to the State and to individuals, and had no hope of release from prison by any other means, they consented to sign the "Cynamahs," or sale-deeds, *for lands which their families had possessed for centuries*. Those of the capitalists who had no friends at Court were made to pay the money for which they had been forced to pledge themselves. . . . The proprietors themselves, plundered of all they had in the world, and without hope of redress, left the country, or took service under our Government or that of Oude, or descended to the rank of day-labourers or cultivators on other estates.

Such is the account given by Sir W. Sleeman of the process by which this great Talookdar acquired his estates—a process which was actively pursued so long as the Native Government of Oude continued to exist. Yet, so detestable was that Government that even the violence and treachery of such men as Dursun Singh, and his son Maun Singh, brought some incidental advantages to the country. If they were robbers, at least they were able to defend their stolen lands from all other robbers weaker than themselves. It is fair to add the account which Sir W. Sleeman gives of the manner in which Maun Singh has administered the ill-gotten gains of his family:—"They have got the lands which they hold by much fraud and violence, but they have done much good to them. They have invited and established in comfort great numbers of the best classes of cultivators from other districts, in which they had ceased to feel secure, and they have protected and encouraged those whom they found on the land."

It must be remembered, however, that the evils for which the dominion of such Talookdars is some compensation, are evils which resulted from a corrupt and feeble Government, and which a strong Government could overcome without the wholesale sacrifice of the rights of others. Sir W. Sleeman puts this very clearly when he says:—

> The greatest benefit conferred upon the lands which they held has been in the suppression of the fearful contests, which used to be perpetual, between the small proprietors of the military classes (among whom the lands had been minutely subdivided by the law of inheritance), about boundaries, and rights to water for irrigation. Many persons used to be killed every year in these contests, and their widows and orphans had to be maintained by the survivors. Now, no such dispute leads to any serious conflict. The landlords are strong, and able to enforce whatever decision is pronounced. They are wealthy, and pay the Government demand punctually. Not a thief or a robber can live or depredate among their tenants. The hamlets are, in consequence, numerous, and peopled by peasantry who seem to live without fear. They adhere strictly to the terms of their engagements with their tenants of all grades, and their tenants all pay their rents punctually.

All this is satisfactory, so far as it goes; and it is a condition of things holding out the strongest temptation to the Government to condone the usurpations of men who are so easily dealt with in their relations with itself. But this is a temptation which ought not to be yielded to beyond a certain point. The Government of India cannot be released, by such considerations, from the obligation of securing, as it has promised to do, all those subordinate rights which Maun Singh and his compeers have spent their lives in overthrowing by violence and fraud.

Far too great stress has been laid on the complicity in rebellion of the village communities of Oude. It was not to be expected that they could resist the influences under which they were placed. In the first place, our mutinous Sepoys were their own brothers and cousins. In the next place, we had not disarmed the Talookdars, and their power remained, therefore, substantially unbroken. It was impossible that the villages could resist it, if they had been ever so disposed to do so. There does not seem, therefore, to be any good reason for sacrificing any proprietary rights which they may be ascertained to have had, in favour of those whose hostility to us was at least as certain, and far more active. It would, indeed, be most inexpedient in India to trace too far back the origin of existing powers. But, in many cases in Oude, the Talookdars were the recent growth of anarchy and fraud. It is well, therefore, that by directions of the Secretary of State in Council,* the special attention of the Indian Government has been called to the danger of a "violent reaction" of opinion in respect to the "failure" of our first Settlement, and to the absolute necessity of so watching and modifying the Settlement with the Talookdars in Oude as to protect, as far as possible, the rights and property of the villagers. This necessity is all the more urgent since Lord Canning took the further step of intrusting some of the Talookdars with a revenue jurisdiction over their estates, and of conferring on them at the same time magisterial powers. This is, indeed, a bold experiment. If it succeeds it will be a great triumph. But to judge whether it succeeds or not we must be vigilant, and if we are not vigilant we shall not be just. We have no right to give such power to such men, unless we not only are willing to believe, but are careful to see, that they do not abuse it.

Closely connected with this "reaction of opinion" in favour of a native aristocracy, stands the measure which Lord Canning took at a somewhat later period on the transmission of inheritance by adoption. The conduct of the native Princes during the contest of 1857-8 was indeed remarkable, and proves, if additional proof were needed, that the insurrection was essentially a mutiny, and nothing else. With few exceptions, they saw clearly that the

* See Oude Papers (July 1861), Despatches of Sir Charles Wood, 24th April, 1860, and 17th August, 1861.

success of the Sepoys would have been merely the success of a lawless soldiery, and that a power before which the British Government should succumb would be a power beside which they themselves could not stand an hour. Their weakness, indeed, made their fidelity in some cases of comparatively little value. The only one within the limits of British India who had any considerable military force, the Maharajah of Gwalior, was unable to restrain his Army from joining the mutineers. This, however, it may be fairly said, was more our fault than his, because his troops were a Contingent under the old subsidiary system, and virtually formed part of the Army of Bengal. The friendly attitude assumed by the Government of the Nizam in the South of India was the most important aid which we derived from any native State.

But it is to be recollected that the infection of the Mutiny never reached the Presidencies of Madras or of Bombay; and, on the whole, it may be said that the tendency of native States really powerful and really independent, is a point on which the events of the Mutiny cast no additional light. It was well for us that there was no native State, either within or beyond our borders, which was sufficiently powerful and sufficiently independent to be tempted by the immense opportunity which our difficulties presented. It was fortunate for us that, before the Great Mutiny broke out, the "Policy of Annexation" had made the Punjaub our own, and that along no British frontier could we any longer see such an Army watching us as the Army of old Runjeet Singh. It was fortunate, too, that within our own external boundary we had no native Prince to deal with in the position which had once been occupied by Holkar, or Scindia, or Tippoo. We had to deal with many native "States," but with not one native "Power." This makes all the difference. Those who talk of the positive advantage of maintaining "native States" should define what they mean. States that are little more than dependent Principalities—Sovereigns that are little more than great nobles,—these may have, under some conditions, an important influence in the peaceful government of so vast a country. But the irresistible logic of events has proved that the safety of our Empire in the East, and of the great interests which that Empire represents, is incompatible with the existence, within the limits of India, of any formidable native Power.

But the direct assistance which had been given to us by some native Chiefs, such as the Maharajah of Puttialla, and the indirect aid which had been rendered by the passive but friendly attitude of others, determined Lord Canning not only to offer personal rewards to these Princes individually, but to take the opportunity of announcing a more definite and a more favourable policy to the whole class than as a rule had prevailed before. It is not true indeed, as has been often alleged, that the policy of the Indian Government had been uniformly or even generally hostile to the old native States. On the contrary, Lord Canning admits that "its orders in dealing with doubtful or lapsed successions have in many instances been liberal and even generous." Lord Dalhousie, who is supposed to represent the view least favourable to native States, had declared that whenever there was a shadow of doubt in respect to the right of succession, that doubt should be ruled in favour of the native Prince. But no general principle had ever been laid down, defining the circumstances under which such doubt would be admitted to exist. Each case as it arose had been dealt with on its separate merits, and the highest authorities were constantly divided as to the abstract principles of Hindoo law, and of Paramount rights, which should be brought to bear upon each decision. The truth is that the practice in India had always varied with the power of the Paramount Authority. Where it was weak the Feudatories had encroached upon it,—where it was strong it had acted on its strength. Runjeet Singh, holding in his hand the reins of a powerful Government, had never recognised the right of adoption among the Chiefs of the Punjaub. Our own policy had varied, because the circumstances of different cases had been various. There is no analogy, for example, between such a "Sovereign" as the Rajah of Sattara, whom we had ourselves set up, and the ancient States which had maintained a relative independence for centuries under the successive conquerors of India. Accordingly, by practice and by precedent, the privilege of transmitting to adopted heirs their own rights of Sovereignty or of Chiefship, had, in respect to many of the old Indian Principalities, been established by our uniform acquiescence. This was the case with the whole group of native States which constitute what is called Rajpootana. Special intimations to the same effect, as a personal reward, had already been given to the great Houses of Scindia, Holkar, Rewah, Puttialla, and others of smaller name. What remained therefore to be done affected only those minor Principalities which are without political power, but which do certainly fulfil far better than the Talookdars of Oude the conditions belonging to a "native aristocracy."

Lord Canning, accordingly, suggested that the time had come when we might adopt and announce some rule, in regard to succession to native States, more distinct than could be found either in our own previous practice or in that of former Paramount Powers of India:—

A time so opportune for the step can never occur again. The last vestiges of the Royal House of Delhi, from which, for our own convenience, we had long been content to accept a vicarious authority, have been swept away. The last pretender to the representation of the Peishwa has disappeared. The Crown of England stands forth the unquestioned Ruler and Paramount Power in all India, and is, for the first time, brought face to face with its feudatories. There is a reality in the suzerainty of the Sovereign of England which has never existed before, and which is not only felt but eagerly acknowledged by the Chiefs. A great convulsion has been followed by such a manifestation of our strength as India had never seen; and if this, in its turn, be followed by an act of general substantial grace to the native Chiefs, over and above the special rewards which have already been given to those whose services deserve them, the measure will be reasonable and appreciated.

Such an act of grace,—and, in my humble opinion, of sound policy, —would be an assurance to every Chief above the rank of Jagheerdar, who now governs his own territory, no matter how small it may be, or where it may be situated, or whence his authority over it may in the first instance have been derived, that the Paramount Power desires to see his Government perpetuated, and that on failure of natural heirs, his adoption of a successor, according to Hindoo law (if he be a Hindoo), and to the customs of his race, will be recognised, and that nothing shall disturb the engagement thus made to him, so long as his House is loyal to the Crown and faithful to the conditions of the treaties or grants which record its obligation to the British Government.

One question immediately rises to our lips on reading this proposal:—What room is left for the discharge of our obligations to the people, as distinguished from the Rulers, of Native States? What is to be done in such a case as Oude? Is disloyalty to ourselves to be the only crime recognised in our dealings with native Governments? Is incompetence, or cruelty, or corruption—the ruin of a country, and the misery of its people—are these to be tolerated, and if tolerated then virtually protected, by the Paramount Power in India? Happily, Lord Canning did not leave in doubt the answer he would give. He says: "The proposed measure will not debar the Government of India from stepping in to set right such serious abuses in a native Government as may threaten any part of the country with anarchy or disturbance, nor from assuming temporary charge of a native State when there shall be sufficient reason to do so. This has long been our practice." Lord Canning reminds us that even Sir George Clerk, who represents the school most favourable to the preservation of native States, had said, in speaking of a particular case in the Hill Country, "The proper punishment for the Paramount State to inflict for gross mismanagement and oppression, such as prevails to a considerable extent in those hills, would be the sequestration of the Chieftaincies." But Lord Canning goes on to say that, in his own opinion, "the penalty of sequestration or confiscation should be used only when the misconduct or oppression is such as to be not only heinous in itself, but of a nature to constitute indisputably a breach of loyalty or of recorded engagement to the Paramount Power." This is the assertion of a principle which is more than doubtful, and which, in extreme cases, it will never be possible to maintain. There was no breach of loyalty towards the British Government on the part of the Rulers of Oude. Except, therefore, upon a higher principle than this, we could not have permanently rescued the people of that distracted country. But surely the duty of protecting the people of India from Rulers who are hopelessly bad, is a duty as least as binding on us as the duty of maintaining our own dominion? Subject to these important reservations, there is much to be said in favour of Lord Canning's policy on the question of Adoption. Liberal as this policy was, towards native Princes, any evil likely to arise from it was greatly modified by two important qualifications—first, that it was specially confined to Princes at that time in the actual exercise of ruling power over their own States; and secondly, that no general intimation was to be made upon the subject, but that a separate notice of the intention of the British Government was to be given to each Chief to whom it was meant that it should individually apply. The first of these limitations excluded the case of all native States in which we had already assumed the powers of Government, even though the nominal Sovereignty of the native Prince might still be maintained: the second limitation secured the power of excluding each particular case in which the expediency of continuing a native "Raj" might be considered doubtful.

The links which bind together all the greater questions of our administration in the East at once drew into discussion, as inseparably connected, the reconstruction of the Indian Army and the re-establishment of Indian Finance. Both had for the time been shattered. Of the great Army of Bengal, numbering in Regular Infantry alone upwards of 74,000 men, only eleven battalions remained with arms in their hands when the Mutiny was quelled. In finance, the condition of the Empire, which before the Mutiny had been good, exhibited at the close of the war an alarming deficit, and a certainty of the debt being more than doubled. But this was not all. Opinions prevailed in respect to the new military system which seemed to render economy impossible, whilst the difficulty of devising new sources of revenue was one among the standard traditions of Indian statesmen. These difficulties, again, tested, in the course of their discussion, the working of the Local Government of India, and led to a material change in its form and structure. On all these matters the solution arrived at belongs, not indeed exclusively to Lord Canning, but wholly to Lord Canning's time; and on each, therefore, it is necessary here to give an outline of the results.

The history of the Councils in India is curious. The original intention of the Company in establishing Councils was to check their Governors; and when Parliament first interfered, by the Act of 1773, the same idea prevailed. The four Councillors of Bengal, as well as the Governor-General, were named by the Act, and the decision of all questions rested with the majority,—the Governor-General having only a vote, and a casting-vote. It was under this system that the famous contest arose between Warren Hastings and Sir Philip Francis, who commanded for a time a majority in the Council. Mr. Pitt's Act of 1784 did not directly put an end to this state of things, but indirectly it did. It had been the death of one member of the Council which had made Hastings suddenly supreme in his own Council; because having one supporter, and his own casting-vote, he could thus always command a majority.* It must have been with some reference to this obvious result, that Pitt's Act of 1784 reduced the number of Councillors from four to three. The consequence, of course, was that if the

* For an account of this event and its consequences, see Lord Macaulay's well-known Essay on Warren Hastings.

Governor-General had even one supporter, he could always command a majority of votes. But beyond this the Act of 1784 did not go. One clause, indeed, was intended to prevent the Governor-General from exercising the power of his majority to such an extent as to muzzle his Council altogether. He could not defeat by adjournment beyond the second time the discussion of "any matter or question" brought forward by a Councillor. Under this system free discussion was at least secured, and in the extreme case of the Governor-General standing absolutely alone, he might be overruled. But two years later Mr. Pitt made important changes, and established the relations between the Governor-General and his Council very much on the footing on which they have ever since remained. In all executive matters the Governor-General was made supreme, although in respect to making "general rules and regulations," he was still left dependent on having at least one supporter. This distinction was not important, because all the real power of the Indian Government lay in executive rather than in legislative action. Practically the Governor-General was supreme, and his authority extended over the minor Presidencies, although in all matters in which this supreme authority was not actually interposed, the Local Governments had full executive and legislative powers. The Act of 1833 first established a "Legislative" as distinct from the Executive Council, by adding a single member to the ordinary Council when sitting for legislative purposes. But the same Act still further concentrated power in the hands of the Governor-General over his own Council, and extinguished any legislative authority in the Local Governments. Even their executive functions were restricted within narrow limits, by their being deprived of all power of independent expenditure.

It was as some remedy for this that the Act of 1853 enlarged the Legislative Council, and added representative members from the minor Presidencies. The Act of 1853 made no change in the powers of the Council, but only in its numbers and composition. But, practically, this enlargement of size,—the habit of holding its sittings or debates in public,—new "standing orders," which simulated the forms of Parliament—and, last not least, an increase of legal members, led to consequences which threatened, at one time, to be a serious embarrassment to Lord Canning's Government. On the whole, however, it is fair to say that the Council, as constituted under the Act of 1853, had not worked ill in matters of legislation. It passed many useful Acts, and the Governor-General had been supported in all the measures he proposed. But the entire incapacity of such a body to assume the functions of a representative assembly for the whole of India, must be apparent at a glance. The change recommended by Lord Canning was adopted by the Home Government, and received the sanction of Parliament in the Session of 1861. It was a change of the highest importance in respect to the Local Government of India. Its object was twofold: first, to break up the relative importance of the Supreme Legislative Council by subdividing its work among a number of separate Bodies; and, secondly, to restore to the minor Presidencies a large share in the executive and legislative powers which had been taken from them by the Act of 1833. The European community of Calcutta has an opportunity of working off its steam in a Local Council for Bengal. The Act specifies a list of Imperial subjects with which these Local Councils cannot interfere. There still remains a Supreme Executive and a Supreme Legislative Council. The members of the Executive Council are each charged with the responsibility of a separate department, and are, in fact, the Cabinet of the Governor-General. In the Legislative Council the nominated members sit for two years only, so as to afford opportunities for change. Room is left for the admission of distinguished natives, who may be selected as really capable of representing the opinions of the native Princes and the native people. But the preponderance of official members is secured; and undue interference with the Executive is prevented by a strict reservation on behalf of the Government of the Initiative in all legislative proceedings. The supremacy, too, of the Governor-General is maintained.

Where a really representative Government is impossible, and where a strong Executive is a necessity, this seems the best principle on which to construct the machinery of the Indian administration. There are no materials in India for any Legislative Body which is not kept in complete subordination to the Governor-General, and above all to the Government at home. A Calcutta Legislature would be the Legislature of a class in its worst and most aggravated form. The "public opinion" of India is virtually the opinion of the small but powerful European community. Its interests are mainly commercial, and its ideas of policy and of law are liable to the bias and insuperable temptations which commercial interests involve. Traditional jealousy made the old servants of the Company a powerful resisting force, and hence the outcry which has been raised against the official class in India. But the years succeeding the Mutiny were years of reaction, and not even Lord Canning's sagacity and firmness were proof against the current which set in so strongly in favour of British settlers in India. In the special penal legislation, which was unfortunately adopted by the Government of India, for the enforcement of indigo-contracts, we have a conclusive proof of the necessity for having a controlling authority at home which shall be competent, vigilant, and strong. The veto which has been put by the Secretary of State in Council on all legislation tending to entangle the Ryots of Bengal in a virtual serfdom to the European Planters has been universally approved at home. The public opinion of the British people and of the British Parliament may on such questions be safely trusted. There never was a more idle fear than the fear so often expressed, of the danger of bringing Indian questions into discussion in Parliament at home. The action and the principles of Parliament have always been generous towards the people of India. The support which Sir Charles Wood and his Council have received from the public voice, in resisting Class Legislation in the Planter interest, is a happy indication that the Government of India under the Crown will not be suffered to degenerate into a Government more commercial in its spirit than the old Company ever was, or less careful of native rights.

A reconstruction of the Army of India has been another consequence of the Great Mutiny. The necessity of maintaining for the future a much larger proportion of European troops, was the first conclusion which every man drew instinctively from that event. Under the impulse of feelings natural after so narrow an escape, the tendency was to overestimate the change which was really needed. Eighty thousand men was the number to which opinion pointed as the minimum required for safety, and at the present moment we have nearly 72,000.* We have seen that when Lord Dalhousie left India the British Force had been reduced to 45,300 men. Whatever doubt there might be as to the exact figure at which it should stand in future, there could be no doubt that it had been dangerously reduced and must be largely reinforced. But how should this reinforcement be contrived? Should it be contrived simply by increasing the number of regiments of the Line stationed in India; or should it be by a large increase in the small local European Force whose service was confined to India,—which had been lately increased by 3,000 men,—but which had not yet been raised to the maximum allowed by law? On this question an irreconcilable difference of opinion arose between a large proportion of Indian statesmen and the Government at home. This was natural enough. The truth is that they looked at the question from two different points of view—

* In 1863.

the one having exclusive reference to Indian interests and Indian traditions, the other having reference to the interests of India only as part of the general interests of the Empire. Lord Dalhousie had felt the risk and the inconvenience of depending so entirely on the Home Authorities for the number of European regiments left at his disposal. The circumstances under which Lord Canning had been placed impressed the same feeling still more deeply on his mind. Considerations different, but not less powerful, in the same direction, told upon the views of the old Indian Services both civil and military. The special and almost exclusive right of those Services to all the great employments connected with the administration of India was the very essence of all that had separated the nominal Government of "The Company" from the Government of the Crown. Already for some years there had been some tendency to encroach upon their privileges, by importing "Queen's Officers" into Indian employments; and the lion's share which these officers had always enjoyed of the highest military commands, had been a long-standing subject of jealousy and of natural complaint. It was instinctively felt that a measure which should largely increase the preponderance in India of the Army of the Line, would place the old local Services at a relative disadvantage. It is not surprising, therefore, that both the Indian Services, and the Governor-General, backed by the Councils both in India and in England, strenuously urged, though on somewhat different grounds, that the reinforcement of the European Army should consist, in large proportion, of an addition to the local Force.

On the other hand, it was equally natural that the Imperial Government should regard this proposal with suspicion. In the first place, that Government was not likely to recognise the doctrine that the free exercise of its discretion on Imperial interests, was a danger against which India, as a separate Government, was required to guard. In the second place, unless the whole minimum

Force of European troops required for the safety of India were to consist of local troops, the Indian Government must still be dependent on the Government at home; yet no man went so far as to make this proposal. In the third place, even the half-measure of making only a moiety of the European Force local in its terms of service, involved a novelty of the most formidable kind And in the fourth place, this new measure,—broadening and deepening the separation between the Army of India and the Army of the Line,—was to be taken at the very time when the two Governments had been brought into nearer and closer union, and when a free interchange of employment between the two Services had been warmly recommended as just in itself, and an indispensable step in military reform.

Here, as well as in the account already given of the Government of "India under Lord Dalhousie," we have had abundant occasion to observe how old debates have been renewed, and old questions of principle revived, during the years passed under our review. This question, in respect to the local European Force, is another instance. Precisely the same proposal had been made—precisely the same tendencies of opinion had been brought to issue—in 1788. The great Minister who had rescued the commerce of the Company and the patronage of India from the political advisers of the Crown, had on the other hand resisted firmly an attempt of the Company to establish in India a powerful European Force distinct from the Army of the Line. This is a very curious subject, and as it is one of which the history seems to have been much forgotten, it may be well to recall here the more important facts.

In the first Charter of the East India Company, in the time of William III., no limitation was placed on the powers of the Company as to the number of European troops which they might raise: they were enabled to raise as many recruits as were found necessary for the "defence of their forts and possessions." At that time it was not foreseen that the East India Company, which was then a mere Trading Association, would one day become a great Territorial Power, and but little importance was consequently attached to their military proceedings. But the moment it was seen that they were likely to be that which they afterwards became, the natural jealousy of the English Parliament and Government was aroused, and statutory limitations were soon placed upon the power of raising European troops. And even long before this precaution was considered necessary, another step, practically even more important, had been taken, which tended to the same effect. Very early in the history of India--in 1754, that is, only four years after the famous defence of Arcot by Clive—the Crown resolved to send troops of the Line to that country; and a detachment of the 39th Regiment, which still bears upon its colours the motto "Primus in Indis," formed no inconsiderable portion of the small European Force which fought at Plassey. In the year 1773, when the Company assumed avowed authority over the Province of Lower Bengal, their European troops amounted in number to 11,468, which appears to be the maximum which had been reached until the other day. In considering, however, the importance of this levy, we must look not only to quantity but also to quality. Now, there is abundant evidence that the East India Company and the Government of India attached but comparatively small importance to their European troops. The truth is that, with the exception of the Artillery corps, respecting which peculiar care was taken from the very earliest time, the local European Army was very ill-organised, and in so inferior a state of discipline that the officers of the Company placed almost their entire reliance upon the Sepoy troops under European command and upon the regiments of the Line. In 1773 Clive declared that our existence in India depended upon the Sepoys commanded by English officers, and that the defence of the country might be entrusted to them alone, supported by a corps of Artillery similarly commanded.

One of the first acts of the new Board of Control erected by Mr. Pitt, in 1784, was to insist on a great reduction of the Company's Forces. Four years later there was an alarm of a renewed contest with the French both in India and in Europe; and it became necessary to strengthen our European garrison in the East. Four more regiments were to be sent. The Company insisted strenuously that the whole of these corps should belong to their own local Europeans: Mr. Pitt as vehemently resisted their desire. There seems to have been nothing that has ever been debated since, which escaped his eagle eye. He resisted the Company avowedly on the ground that the change which was really expedient was a change in precisely the opposite direction,—namely, a change towards a consolidation of the two Armies, and not towards a more effectual separation. He declared that such a consolidation was undoubtedly to be wished for, and that "*sooner or later it must be attempted.*" Mr. Pitt carried his point, though by a smaller majority of the House of Commons than was usual in his first triumphant Ministry. In the same year the maximum of the local European Force was fixed at 12,000 men. This limit was never actually reached; and in 1796 they were reduced to two regiments of five companies,—or, virtually, to one regiment of Infantry in each Presidency. And so matters had remained till, as we have seen, the necessity of withdrawing Line regiments from India to serve in the Russian war had led in 1856 to an Act being passed which raised the maximum of the local European Force from 12,000 to 20,000 men. When the Mutiny broke out, it still only stood at three regiments in each Presidency, or about 9,000 men in all. This was exclusive of the Indian Artillery, which had always been entirely local, and was a force of admirable efficiency. But now the demand made was one of a much more formidable kind. The Military Committee of the Indian Council were of opinion that, of the total European Force to be maintained in India, the whole of the Artillery, three-fourths of the Cavalry, and two-thirds of the Infantry should belong exclusively to the Local Service. Lord Canning himself urged that on no consideration should the proportion be less than one-half. That this should have been thought expedient by Indian officers is intelligible enough. But they made a great historical mistake when they argued, as Sir James Outram did, that an amalgamation of the local European Force with the Army of the Line "would be an organic change in that military system under which India has been won and kept."

Whatever might be said for the proposal that one-half of the whole European Force in India should be a local Force, one thing at least was clear,—that such a measure would have been a far more "organic change in the military system by which India had been won and kept," than the opposite measure which had been contemplated by Mr. Pitt,—viz., that of dispensing with local Europeans altogether, and officering the Native Army on some system which would consolidate the two Services instead of keeping them apart. Lord Canning did not affirm, as some others did, that the comparatively small Force of local Europeans which had been hitherto maintained had formed any principal element in our Indian military system. On the contrary, he admitted that, "forming as they did a very small portion of the Indian Army, they had been until lately almost overlooked by their successive Commanders-in-Chief." Lord Cornwallis had declared, in 1786, that with the exception of the corps of Artillery, he had nothing but the King's regiments of the Line "that deserved the name of an European Force." In more recent times the Company's regiments had indeed borne a high character in the field, and had taken a brilliant part in all our Indian wars; but still the Duke of Wellington had borne emphatic testimony to the relative inferiority of their military discipline. This, indeed, was admitted by Lord Canning, and to some extent by the most distinguished Indian officers themselves. The risk of mutiny among European troops in India is not, perhaps, a formidable danger: it was, however, constantly urged as a plea for a divided Army. But, in so far as this danger could be contemplated at all, it undoubtedly told against a large Force separated from the Army of the Line. Without anticipating positive mutiny, it is certain that a powerful Army, having special relations with India and the native troops—watching with envious eyes every command given to officers of the Line, and trained in a spirit of jealousy towards the "Horse-Guards," —or, in other words, towards the authority of the Crown —would have been a serious embarrassment to the Government.

The Cabinet of Lord Palmerston therefore rejected this proposal of the Indian Services. Only one alternative remained—the "consolidation" which Mr. Pitt had foreseen to be inevitable. There was all the more reason to adopt this course, since several of the measures involved in it had been already urgently recommended as in themselves most desirable, if not absolutely required. Such, for example, was the formation of a "Staff Corps," from which, instead of from the regiments, might be drawn the officers employed throughout India in the infinite variety of duties belonging to the administration of the country. We have seen that this measure had been pointed to by Lord Dalhousie as the only remedy for an evil which involved serious danger to the discipline and fidelity of the Army. Sir Henry Lawrence had urged its adoption as the most important conclusion to which he had come on military reform. Not less general was the concurrence of opinion that eligibility for the Staff Corps, or for a Staff employment, ought not to be confined to officers of the local Service, but should be open also to qualified officers of the Line; and Lord Canning expressly recommended that there should be a free exchange between both Services. But this is "consolidation" or "amalgamation." It was surely more consistent with this system that native troops should be the only local Force, and that the whole European Army should belong to the Army of the Line, and be available for the general service of the Empire. The only real danger of the amalgamation has reference to the officering of the Native Army. This must always continue to be a matter of the very first importance. It would be a serious evil indeed if, under the new system, the old school of officers who organised and commanded corps belonging to the native races, should be broken up. But the intention of the Staff Corps is to constitute a body from which such men may continue to be drawn—men devoting themselves to the Indian local service, and casting in their lot with it. There seems to be no reason why the same encouragements and the same prospects of distinction should not tell as strongly in favour of that service as it has ever done. This, however, must be watched with care.

It marks how small was the amount of legal change required, and how little it altered the statutory system of Indian Government, that the "Amalgamation Act," passed in 1860, was an Act of a single clause, simply providing that Europeans should no longer be recruited for local service in India. All other changes have been effected by the ordinary action of the Executive Government: they have had no necessary connection either with the extinction of the Company's nominal position, nor with the "Amalgamation Act." They would have been equally competent to the Court of Directors and the old Board of Control, and most of them have been determined by considerations of efficiency and economy, as well as by the light thrown on the defects of our military system by the Great Mutiny of 1857-8.

Concurrently with these questions as to how the Army of India should be reorganised, arose the question, not less difficult, how the Finance of India should be re-established? The effects of the Mutiny may be told in a few words. In the year before the outbreak the revenue and the expenditure had been almost exactly equal. During the three years 1858–9–60 the aggregate deficiencies exceeded 30 millions. In 1857 the capital of the Indian public debt had stood at (about) 59½ millions. In February 1860 it exceeded 90 millions. Even at that date the Mutiny had added above 30 millions to the Indian debt, which has now farther risen to about 100 millions. But if the effect was alarming, at least the cause was simple, and the remedy obvious. The cause was enormous military expenditure, and the remedy must be mainly, if not exclusively, military reduction. In 1856–7 the total military charges had been below 11½ millions; in 1858–9 they were upwards of 21 millions. One-half of the whole British Army was quartered on the revenues of India, and the Native Force, instead of being smaller, was vastly larger than it had been before the Mutiny arose. The European troops of all arms amounted to 112,000 men, whilst the native troops, including the irregular levies and the military police, had risen to the enormous figure of 310,000 men—an excess of about 50,000 men over the Native Force as it had stood in 1856.

But the Government of India found itself not only in the face of an enormous deficit, but in the face of opinions on its future military system which would have rendered escape from that deficit impossible. The Military Commission appointed in this country to enquire into the subject were unanimous that the number of European troops to be kept in India should not be less than 80,000 men; and further, that the proportion this Force should bear to the native troops should never be less than one to three, and in many districts should be one to two. The Native Army must therefore be from 180,000 to 200,000 men. Although this purely professional opinion was at once perceived to be impracticable by the Government at home, yet it was hard to see how retrenchment could be carried so far as to restore an equal balance to the Indian Exchequer. Two millions annually—on which there could be no reduction—had been then already added to the expenditure on the interest of the debt alone ; so that, unless the military establishment could be reduced even below the amount at which it had stood before the Mutiny, it was impossible that, with the existing revenue, the Government could escape from a position of permanent embarrassment.

It was under the pressure of this difficulty and alarm that the Government of India was compelled to consider the question of new taxes. But it could not consider this question without bringing under review the whole of its existing system of revenue. Accordingly every part of that system has been eagerly discussed—tested by every kind of theory, criticised by every kind of interest—not without large results on its actual condition, and still larger promise of reforms to come.

In estimating the ability of a people to bear new taxes, it is a common mode of stating the case, to divide the total revenue by the number of the population, and to represent the burden they bear as so much per head. The result obtained is then compared with the result of a similar calculation in respect to England, or some other country. The process looks very neat, but, like many other processes of the same kind, it is entirely worthless. The oppressiveness of a burden does not depend on its absolute weight, but on its relation to the strength of the back which is required to bear it. The rate per head of taxation which is light to the prosperous farmers of England, would ruin the cottier peasantry of Connaught. It is idle to compare the taxes of two nations unless we have first compared their wealth. Yet this sort of comparison was common in discussing the possibility of new Indian taxes. And there was another fallacy not less deceiving. One-half—in round numbers—of the whole revenues of India was the revenue derived from land.* This, it was argued,

* In 1858–59 the total revenue was 36,060,788*l*: of this the land revenue was 18,123,659*l*.

was no "tax"—it was only rent. But as regards the ability of those who pay this revenue to bear new taxes, it matters nothing whether their payment be called a "rent," or whether it be called a "tax." That ability must be determined not by the name given to the portion of his substance which a man pays to the State, but by the amount which is left to him after that payment has been made. As regards the power of a people to bear new burdens, it is quite the same whether they be overrented or overtaxed. Now, what was the condition generally of the Indian Ryot—of the actual cultivator of the soil? Was it a condition of comfort and comparative wealth, or of poverty and comparative depression?

There could be but one answer to these questions. Our Government in India had derived from its predecessors the dangerous inheritance of a landlord's power and a landlord's right over a gigantic territory cultivated by millions of men. The best and wisest of our statesmen had been staggered by the enormous difficulties which attended the administration of such powers in the hands of Government. But amidst every variety of theory and of plan in respect to "Settlements" of land, one idea, one principle of policy, had been making steady way, and every hope of comfort and of progress was identified with its extended application; and that was to make our assessments generally lower, and for longer periods. In other words, experience had taught us that, generally speaking, our rent-taxes, or our tax-rents, were too high, and our people were too poor. It was therefore universally conceded that, whatever new taxes should be levied, they should be taxes affecting as little as possible the cultivators of the soil. But whilst our revenue system bore heavily on the Ryot, it bore very lightly on other classes of the community, and there were some—and these the richest—who contributed little or nothing to the necessities of the State. The only tax of any importance which bore on the general consumption of the people was the Salt Tax; this, it was thought, could bear an increase. The Customs contributed less than one-fifteenth of the revenues of India; they also could bear an increase. But, above all, there was no tax on the incomes of great proprietors, or of capitalists, or of merchants; there could be no reason for this exemption. Accordingly, resort has been had to all these sources of revenue. Others were proposed but were subsequently abandoned, and the energetic protest of Sir Charles Trevelyan against them all must be fresh in the recollection of our readers. That protest was of great value, in so far as it insisted that reduction could be carried very much further than was contemplated at the time. But if new taxes were required at all, the establishment of an income-tax was a just and a valuable addition to the revenues of India, producing about £1,200,000. The total revenues of India have risen from about 37 millions, at which they stood before the Mutiny, to about 44 millions for 1863. If the charges on account of the railway system be excluded, the expenditure is less than the revenue by above a million; and even taking those charges into account, the deficit for the year 1863–4 is likely to be small. The new taxes, therefore, have been doing well, and their value will be infinitely enhanced if they can be used, as Sir Robert Peel used new taxes here—not to support an extravagant expenditure, but to help the Government in reducing taxes which are more oppressive—more obstructive to the increase and accumulation of wealth.

This brings us to the question, which perhaps more than any other affects the condition of the people of India, and which has been brought to an issue of immense importance by the action of Lord Canning's Government. When Lord Stanley was at the India Office in 1858-9, he had directed an enquiry into the expediency of making the Land Revenue of India redeemable by the occupiers or proprietors of the soil. The idea which lies at the root of this proposal is that the land revenue, as it has been hitherto established, is a barrier to improvement. This is true. But is there no remedy for this except the total alienation of the Land-tax? Affecting as it does the great mass of a population which is mainly agricultural, the kind of modification which is required is that which will most directly reach that mass, and give new motives to their industry. Is the power of redeeming their land assessment —of buying it up altogether—is this an offer which it is likely the Indian Ryot can accept? Living too generally from hand to mouth, having no capital except what he borrows from others, he has no means of purchase at his command. There are others who might take advantage of the offer; these would be either the wealthy "Zemindars," the large native proprietors, or more generally the European Planters. It has indeed been always avowedly in the interest of this class that the proposal has been made. Lord Stanley's suggestion was expressly made with special reference to "the importance of affording all possible encouragement to the employment of British capital, skill, and enterprise in the development of the material resources of India."

But important as this object undoubtedly is, it is not more important than the encouragement of the capital and industry of the natives. Little would be gained by a measure which tends to favour the European Planter, if it does not equally tend to favour the great bulk of that class from which the land revenue is derived. It is on them that the bad effects of our system had been operating most widely and most severely. It is in their interest and to their relief that any reform of the land revenue must be directed, if it is to tell upon the future of India, or add quickly to the wealth and comfort of the people. Of late years we had been moving in the right direction. We had been making our Settlements more moderate in amount, and, above all, longer in duration—the term generally given being thirty years. The Ryots were becoming, as it were, holders of long leases, instead of tenants from year to year. Every step in this direction had been attended with success—a rising revenue, and an improving people. Still, the power which the Government retained of raising its demand indefinitely at the end of the lease or period of settlement, operated to check improvement; and it is notorious that towards the close of the terms it has been the constant practice of the Ryot not only to relax his industry, but purposely to deteriorate the value and productiveness of his land. A system which leads to such results is self-condemned.

But the remedy for this must be as wide as the evil—not a remedy which would apply only here and there to a few English Planters or a few wealthy Zemindars. Accordingly, some misgiving as to the partial operation of a power of redemption, had been present to the mind of the Secretary of State in 1859, for his despatch concluded with these words: "I particularly request that in any suggestions or recommendations which you may submit to me, you will be especially careful not to confine them to such as may be calculated for the exclusive advantage of European settlers, and which cannot be equally participated in by the agricultural community generally." It is fair, however, to Lord Canning's Government to remember that the only measure actually suggested by the Secretary of State was that the land-tax should be made redeemable. Lord Stanley had indeed observed, with truth, that "the permission to redeem the land-tax can operate only, in so far as the people may avail themselves of such permission, *as a permanent settlement of the land-tax at its present amount.*" But no means were pointed out whereby the advantages of this permanent settlement could be secured by any except the few who could afford to buy it. A plan of selling the land-tax was accordingly announced by the Indian Government, somewhat hastily, as an adopted measure.

Partial as it must have been in its operation, under any circumstances, it was rendered still more partial by its avowedly experimental character, and its limitation to a small proportion of the land (10 per cent.) in each collectorate. The Home Government has now wisely decided to set aside this experiment, and to enter upon a much larger reform—one which goes to the very root of the whole matter, and inaugurates a new era in the Finance of India. Our Land Settlements are in future to be made,—not from year to year, not for a term of years,—but once and for ever. The cultivator of the soil is to be sure that he will reap all the fruits of his own industry, that the demands of the State can never absorb more than a fixed amount of the produce of the soil, and that all he can raise beyond that amount will be his own. This great measure has been taken with the cordial assent of a large majority of the Indian Council.* We hear a great deal sometimes of the intricacy of Indian tenures, and of the difference between the ideas of ownership which prevail there and those to which we are accustomed in Europe. But there are some principles which are of universal application, because they rest on the nature of man, and can never cease to operate on the Wealth of Nations. One of these is the close connection which obtains between the progress of industry and the certainty of enjoying its results. This is one principle which tells in favour of a "Permanent Settlement;" and there is another which tells not less decisively against the only objection which is ever raised. The State, it is sometimes said, sacrifices by a Permanent Settlement its interest in the natural increase of the value of the soil. But the wealth of a Government, if it is such as deserves the name, lies in the wealth of its people. The notion of its having a separate interest of its own is a barbarous and Oriental notion. Nothing is lost, but much is gained,

* The dissents of the minority, together with an admirable paper by Sir John Lawrence in favour of the measure, have been presented to Parliament (July 21, 1862), and afford an excellent view of the whole question.

when a Government yields to its people that which will stimulate their industry, and tend to the accumulation of their wealth.

But by the time this decision had been taken, Lord Canning's career was closed. Long before he left India the relation in which his character had stood to the memorable events of 1857 came to be universally recognised by a grateful country. How often, in the lives of remarkable men, are we tempted to wish that such recognitions had been yielded sooner! But if the rarer virtues received always, and at once, the homage of the multitude, those virtues would themselves be less. The power of resisting passion is the power of resisting that which carries before it other men. They cannot see it as it is, till their own vision has been cleared, and the balance of their mind restored. Enough if they see it then, and are eager to thank the man whose character is greater than their own. When Lord Canning landed in England there was no honour which he might not have had at the public hands. The modesty of his disposition would, probably, have led him to avoid such honours at any time. But, besides this, his health was broken by work, by climate, and by severe affliction. Within a few weeks of his arrival, the grave of an illustrious Father was opened to receive the body of an illustrious Son. His funeral was attended by a large number of the men most distinguished in public life, both of this generation and of that which is nearly gone. There were there colleagues of the Elder Canning, who had seen with pleasure, and with curious surprise, the very different but not less valuable qualities which replaced in his son the brilliancy and genius of their own early friend. There were there some who had known Lord Canning chiefly as the close political follower of Lord Aberdeen, and who recognised in the temper of his mind the same spirit of generous resistance against all forms of popular injustice. There were there many of Lord Canning's companions in school and college life, to whom his great reputation was no surprise, because they had long known his safe sagacity and his manly judgment. There were there others who, with no mixture of personal feeling, represented only the universal sorrow of the Sovereign and the People. That sorrow came from the public heart, and was the deeper because it touched also the public conscience. All men felt that Westminster Abbey was receiving that day, under its venerable pavement, the remains of one who had done much to restore, and—better still—to justify, our dominion in the East: who, at a time when it was sadly needed, had exhibited to India and the world some of the finest virtues of the English character, and in doing so had shed new lustre on the English name.